Cooking for Sugar

SPOILING YOUR PUP WITH
DOGLICIOUS
HOMEMADE TREATS

ROSALYN ACERO

ISBN 978-1-63353-403-2

"Food is symbolic of love when words are inadequate."

—Alan lan D. Wolfelt

Table of Contents

Cooking For Sugar

Why I Make Homemade
Treats For My Pup

When I was young, I enjoyed helping out baking special treats, and I had an aspiration to be a pastry chef. Now, I continue to bake as a hobby inspired by Sugar. One of Sugar's secret for having a long life is her healthy diet. Due to Sugar's allergies, I'm selective on treating her with store bought commercial dog treats. Mostly, I treat Sugar with homemade healthy dog treats with superfood ingredients. I prefer to make simple dog treats in small quantity to preserve its freshness and provide Sugar variety of flavors. I love when I can make a recipe that I can share with Sugar. I'm able to showcase my creativity too - combining ingredients and presentation. The best part about making homemade dog treats for Sugar is the look on her face, "Woofs, for more treats!"

The Benefits of Love

Why You Should Make Homemade Dog Treats

Making dog treats is not as complicated or time-consuming as you may think; plus it provides your dog many benefits. While not all commercial dog treats have the potential to be bad for your dog, homemade dog treats are a better option because you are in control of everything and because you put your love behind it. When baking, you can easily avoid unsafe additives and other ingredients that you've probably never heard of or even know how to pronounce. This total control of ingredients is perfect for any pup who might be allergic or on a specific diet.

Making your own dog treats is not only easy, but it can also be fun. Using simple ingredients you probably already have in your kitchen, you can whip up dog treats in minutes. You can also incorporate superfood fruits and vegetables to give your treats extra nutrients.

Cooking for your dog is also a tremendous opportunity to get better acquainted. It allows you to be creative and experiment with different ingredients and recipes that fit your dog's health. Your dog deserves the best!

A Happier and Healthier Friend

Why You'll Never Go Back To Processed Treats

Just like cooking your own meals is cheaper than buying takeout, making your dog treats will save you money as well. Set aside some dog friendly ingredients you use for cooking to make treats for your dog. Dog treats made in small batches provide a variety of flavors, and your dog will appreciate the freshness.

Incorporate superfoods into your dog treat recipes. The same superfoods you eat for the antioxidants, vitamins and extra nutrients are just as good for your dog. It's true. Most of the foods you eat to keep your heart and body healthy can be fed to your dog. Here are 10 superfoods that you may already be eating, that are perfect to share with your dog.

#1

Kale

This leafy green veggie is packed full of vitamins like A, E, C and K, as well beta carotene, calcium, potassium and magnesium. It offers a good source of antioxidants and even helps detox the liver. With 5 grams of fiber per serving, kale can help keep your dog's digestive system working right.

#2

Broccoli

This nutrient-rich vegetable contains fiber to keep your dog's tummy running right. It is also rich in nutrients like calcium, vitamin C, potassium and protein. Broccoli is said to be anti-inflammatory and can help keep eyes and skin healthy.

#3

Carrots

These crunchy, sweet veggies are a great snack for your pooch! While you may know that carrots are good for eye health, they are also good for your heart, teeth and lungs. Carrots contain vitamins like A, vitamin C and vitamin K, as well as vital nutrients like beta carotene. They also contain many B vitamins and phosphorus which can help give your dog added energy. Carrots make a great snack; can be served raw or cooked.

#4

Pumpkin

Pumpkin is high in beta carotene. It also contains lots of vitamin C and potassium, and the soluble fiber found in pumpkin can help maintain a healthy and happy digestive system. Pumpkin can aid to help a dog's upset stomach.

#5

Sweet Potatoes

Sweet Potatoes are another source of dietary fiber, and high in vitamin A, a heart-healthy vitamin. Sweet potatoes will help keep your dog's coat looking shiny and immune system healthy.

#6

Blueberries

Whether you buy them frozen or get them fresh, blueberries make a great treat for your dog. They are loaded with antioxidants, a source of vitamins E, C and Magnesium. Blueberries can be used as a snack, and are a great treat alternative.

#7 Apples

Who doesn't like apples? They're sweet and crunchy, and they're delicious! Apples contain vitamin C, vitamin K, fiber and calcium. Just make sure to remove the seeds before serving up the apples to your dog. The seeds are poisonous and will cause an upset stomach.

#8

Bananas

Bananas are a great source of potassium, which is necessary for muscles, nerves and enzymes to function properly. It also helps maintain the proper fluid balance in your dog.

#9

Salmon

Fatty fish like salmon is a great source of omega 3 and omega 6 fatty acids. These fatty acids are essential to reducing the effects of allergies. Fatty fish also help keep your dog's coat looking shiny, and reduces skin itching. For dogs with arthritis, these fatty acids can help reduce inflammation and arthritic pain. Salmon is also a great source of protein and other vitamins, making it a great addition to any dog treat recipe.

#10

Chia

Chia seeds have gotten a lot of buzz lately from the health food scene. This superfood is a great source of fiber and is a complete protein, which means it has the right proportion of all nine amino acids. It is also a good plant source of omega 3 fatty acids, calcium and antioxidants, and a natural source of energy.

Just as these superfoods are great for you, they are just as good for your dog! Explore ways to add these superfoods to your dog treat recipes.

Recipes

The Sunday Morning Banana Blueberry Pancakes

Ingredients

1 ripe banana
1/2 cup of blueberries
2 tablespoon of coconut flour
1 egg
1 teaspoon of honey (optional)
coconut oil to coat pan

Directions

In a bowl, break up the banana into chunks then add the blueberries. Using a fork, thoroughly mash the banana chunks and blueberries until almost smooth.

Whisk the egg then pour over the banana. Stir until the egg is completely combined. Add gradually the coconut flour and honey. Stir until semi-smooth batter.

Heat coconut oil over medium heat. Use a circle or dog bone cookie cutter and place place the batter inside. cook each side for about a minute (depending on the thickness).

Topping

Plain yogurt with fresh blueberries juice (mashed blueberries)

Tip

Don't over mash the banana and blueberries.

Say Cheese Bars

Ingredients

1 cup of rice flour

1/4 cup of extra thick rolled oats

1/3 cups of cheese (cheddar)

1/4 grated carrots

11/3 tablespoon of fresh finely grated parsley

1 egg

3 tablespoon of water

Directions

In a bowl, combine the flour and oats. Then, add the cheese, carrots and parsley. Stir well.

In a separate bowl, whisk the egg and add the water. Gradually add to the dry ingredients and mix well until the ingredients are thoroughly combined.

Place the dough on a well-floured surface. Knead the dough until smooth. Roll the dough to a 1/4-inch thickness and then cut into rectangular shapes.

Mini Turkey Mutt'in

Ingredients

1 cup of cooked ground turkey (seasoned with turmeric)
1/3 cup of brown rice flour
1/2 cup of spinach
1/3 cup of cauliflower
1/4 cup of cheese
1 egg
1 teaspoon of coconut oil

Directions

In a blender, place the cauliflower, spinach and cheese. Process on low speed until smooth. In a bowl, whisk the egg, add blended spinach, cauliflower and cheese, then coconut oil and turkey. Gradually add the flour and stir the mixture until well blended. Pour the mixture into a mini silicon muffin cups. Bake at 350 degrees for 30 - 45 minutes. Makes 12 cups.

Nutty Cheese Donut Biscuits

Ingredients

1/2 cup of coconut flour
1/3 cup oats flour
1/3 cup of cheddar cheese
1 tablespoon of coconut oil
1 teaspoon of honey
1 teaspoon of chia seeds
2 tablespoon of water

Directions

In a bowl, combine all the ingredients and stir well. Pour the mixture in a donut silicon mold. Bake at 350 degrees for 30 to 45 minutes. Makes 8 medium size donut biscuits.

Optional Topping

Greek yogurt and cheddar cheese.

Green and Nutty and Apple and Berry

Ingredients

1 1/2 cups of flour
1 cup of fresh spinach
1 granny smith apple
(cut in cubes with skin)
1/4 cup of peanut butter
1/4 cup of blueberries

Directions

In a mixer, blend together spinach and apple. Add the peanut butter and blueberries; mix until completely combined. Gradually add the flour and stir until the dough starts to come together. (Dough will be sticky.)

Place the dough on a well-floured surface. Knead the dough until smooth. Roll the dough to a 1/4-inch thickness and cut out the treats using a bone cookie cutter.

Bake at 350 degrees for 30 to 45 minutes or until golden brown. Makes 24 treats.

Dried Chewbanana

Ingredients

bananas

Optional

lemon
honey

Directions

Peel and cut the banana in half length-wise. Lay slices on a cookie sheet lined with parchment paper or silicon mat. Optional: Brush each slice with lemon juice

Bake at 210 degrees for 1.5 hours. Let it cool and drizzle some honey (optional).

Frosty Berry Bone Parfait

Ingredients

1 tablespoon of greek yogurt
1 tablespoon of plain yogurt
2 teaspoon of fresh blackberries juice (3 pieces of blackberries)
4 x-small pieces of strawberries
1 teaspoon of homemade toasted coconut honey oats

Directions

As a mold, use a 31/4-inch bone cookie cutter. Place on a flat surface, such as a glass plate. Pour 1 tablespoon of Greek yogurt. Freeze it for about an hour. Add 2 teaspoon of the fresh blackberries juice. Freeze 20 to 30 minutes. Place little pieces of strawberries over blackberry juice, then pour 1 tablespoon of plain yogurt on top. Freeze for 20 minutes. Place 1 teaspoon homemade Toasted Coconut Honey Oats (see recipe below) on top. Freeze another 10 to 15 minutes.

Toasted Coconut Honey Oats

Mix 11/2 tablespoon of coconut oil and 1/4 cup rolled. In a skillet, toast over medium-high heat 5 to 7 minutes, until oats are golden brown. Remove from heat and mix in 1 teaspoon honey.

Elvis' Peanut Butter & Banana Frozen Donuts

Ingredients

1 banana
1 tablespoon of peanut butter

Directions

Cut the banana into round pieces (7-9 pieces, depending the size of the banana). Make a small hole in the middle of each round piece. Fill each round piece with peanut butter. Serve as is or freeze for about 1-2 hours before serving.

Salmon Carrot Bone Oats

Ingredients

1 1/4 cup of flour
1 cup of oats
1/2 cup of salmon;
cooked salmon
(seasoned with turmeric)
1/2 cup of grated carrots
1 egg
2 teaspoon of oil
1 cup of water

Directions

Combine all the dry ingredients. Gradually stir whisked egg with oil and water. Adjust the liquid as necessary to make a stiff dough.

Place the dough on a well-floured surface. Knead the dough until smooth. Roll the dough to a 3/8-inch thickness and cut out the treats using a bone cookie cutter.

Bake at 350 for 45 to 60 minutes until thorough dry and golden brown. Tip: Bake at a lower temperature and longer for extra crunchy treat.

Sweet Paw-tatoes

Ingredients

1 large sweet potato
1 tablespoon coconut oil
1/2 teaspoon of turmeric

Directions

Combine coconut oil and turmeric. Cut the sweet potato lengthwise. Then coat it with coconut and turmeric mixture.

Spread the seasoned sweet potatoes in an even layer on a baking sheet. Bake the potatoes at 400 degrees. stirring occasionally, until tender and golden brown, about 20 to 30 minutes.

Kale Cocktail

1/2 cup of kale
1/3 of granny smith
apple with skin
1/4 cup of broccoli
florets
1/4 grilled pineapple

Makes 12 cubes and about a cup.

In a blender, mix all the ingredients. Pour mixture into an ice tray or silicon mold, then freeze it. Serve it as is or blend it again for frosty paw kale-ada.

Creamy Banana Ice Cream

Ingredients

ripe bananas

Directions

Cut the bananas into small chunks then freeze for 3 hours or 24 hours (recommended).

Using a blender or food processor, blend the frozen bananas. Mixture will be crumbly at first, then mixture have a creamy consistency.

Banana Strawberry Ice Cream

Ingredients

ripe bananas
strawberries

Directions

Cut the bananas into small chunks and cut the strawberry sin help. Freeze for 3 hours or 24 hours (recommended).

Using a blender or food processor, blend the frozen bananas and stawberries. Mixture will be crumbly at first, then will have a creamy consistency.

Watermelon Chia Berry

Ingredients

1/4 cup of chunks of
watermelon
1/4 cup of blueberries
1 table spoon of chia seeds

Directions

In a blender, blend all the ingredients. Pour the liquid into a ice cube mold and freeze it for an hour.

Blueberry Cluster Oats

Ingredients

1/2 cup of rice flour
1/4 of extra thick rolled oats
1/4 cup of blueberries
1/3 cup of mashed sweet potato
1 egg
2 tablespoon of honey

Directions

In a bowl, mash the blueberries then add the sweet potato, egg, and stir well. In a separate bowl, combine the rice flour with the rolled oats and gradually add into blueberry mixture. Once thoroughly mixed, pour the honey over the oat mixture. Stir Well.

Pour the oat mixture onto the baking sheet and spread it out into an even layer. Bake at 350 degrees for 20 to 30 minutes until the clusters are light golden in color. Let it cool at room temperature. Use a teaspoon and your hand.

Fruity Pup-sicles

~1 1/2 banana
2 strawberries
handful of blueberries
3 cubes of watermelon
1/4 mango
ice cubes

use fun ice molds

1) Combine 1/2 banana with 1 ice cubes in a blender and blend until smooth. Pour into a mold. Place in freezer for at least 2 hours.

2) Combine 1/4 banana, watermelon with 1 ice cube in a blender and blend until smooth. Pour into a mold. Place in freezer for at least 2 hours.

3) Repeat 2) process to make the strawberry, blueberry, and mango.

Mini Banana Bagel

Ingredients

1 ripe banana
1/4 cup flour
1 egg
1 teaspoon of honey

Directions

In a bowl, thoroughly mash the banana until almost smooth. Whisk the egg then pour over the banana. Stir until the egg is completely combined. Add gradually the flour and honey. Mix well until the ingredients are thoroughly combined.

Pup-kin Pie

Ingredients

Directions

Pie Crust

1/3 cup flour
1/4 cup steel oats
1/4 cup unsweetened
apple sauce (or blend
an apple in a blender)
1 egg

In a bowl, combine all pie crust ingredients and stir well. Fill in the sides only of a mini pumpkin silicon mold. Bake at 350 degrees for 15 minutes. Makes 8 about 12 mini apple pumpkin crusts.

Filling

1/2 cup pumpkin puree
1/2 teaspoon cinnamon

Pour the pumpkin filling on each crust. Bake at 350 degrees for 15 minutes.

Mini Banana Chia Sandwich Ice Cream

Ingredients

1 frozen banana (cut into small chunks)
10 banana cookies
1/2 teaspoon chia seeds

1 ripe banana (cut into small cubes)
1/4 cup flour
1/4 cup steel cut oats
1 egg
1 teaspoon of coconut oil

Directions

Banana Chia Ice Cream

Using a blender or food processor, blend the frozen bananas. Mixture will be crumbly at first, then mixture have a creamy consistency. Stir in chia seeds.

Banana Cookies

Combine the flour and oats. Gradually stir whisked egg with coconut oil. Then, the ripe banana cubes. Stir until the dough starts to come together. (Dough will be sticky.) Place the dough on a well-floured surface. Knead the dough until smooth. Roll the dough to a 1/4-inch thickness and cut out the treats using a mini round cookie cutter. Bake at 350 degrees for 30 to 45 minutes or until golden brown.

Assemble the mini Banana Chia Sandwich Ice Cream. Take a small scoop of Banana Chia Ice Cream and sandwich it between two Banana Cookies. Freeze the sandwiches for an hour or overnight.

Sweet Potatoes Chips by the River

Ingredients

1/2 cup cooked salmon seasoned with numeric
1/2 cup mashed sweet potato
1/2 cup of flour
1/3 cup of brown rice flour
1 egg
1 tablespoon flax seed

Directions

In a bowl combine the flour and flax seed.

In a separate bowl, combine the salmon and sweet potato. Whisk the egg then pour over. Stir until the egg is completely combined. Gradually the combined flour and flaxseed mixture. mix well until the ingredients are thoroughly combined.

Place the dough on a well-floured surface. Knead the dough until smooth. Roll the dough to a 1/4-inch thickness and then cut into small squares.

Bake at 350 degrees for 30 - 45 minutes. Makes 32 squares.

Thanksgiving Burger Bone

Ingredients

Directions

Pumpkin Bone Bun

2 tablespoon pumpkin
puree
2 tablespoon flour
2 teaspoon of ginger
water (or plain water)

In a bowl combine all the Pumpkin Bone
Bun ingredients. Stir until the egg is
completely combined. Pour the mixture
into a bone cookie cutter. Only fill in the
cookie cutter 1/2 Mixture makes 2 bone
buns. Bake at 350 degrees for 20 minutes
or until golden brown.

Turkey Bone Burger

2 tablespoon cooked
turkey seasoned with
turmeric
1/2 teaspoon shredded
cheddar cheese
finely chopped broccoli
floret
1 tablespoon of whisk egg
coconut oil to coat pan

Combine the turkey, shredded cheese and
whisk egg. Sprinkle some finely chopped
broccoli florets. Heat coconut oil over
medium heat. Using dog bone cookie
cutter and place place the turkey mixture
inside. Cook each side for about 15 seconds
minute.

Assemble the Turkey Burger Bone with the
Pumpkin Bone Bun.

Midnight Sushi

Ingredients

1 soy sushi wrapper
1/3 cup of cooked medium grain rice
1 tablespoon cooked salmon seasoned with turmeric
1 small piece of cucumber (cut lengthwise)

Directions

Lay the Bamboo sushi-roll mat on a cutting board with bamboo strips going horizontally from you. Place a saran wrap on top of the mat. Place the soy wrapper on top of the plastic wrap. Spread a thin layer of rice on the soy wrapper. Leave approximately one inch of uncovered nori at each end.

Make a soft indentation in the middle. Then fill in with salmon and cucumber. Roll the sushi with the bamboo mat. With a wet knife cut the roll into desired size.

Bacon for Breakfast, Lunch and Dinner

Ingredients

1/2 cup shredded cheese
1/2 slice cooked bacon
(finely diced)
1/3 coconut flour
1/4 rolled oats
1 egg

Directions

In a bowl, combine all the cheese, bacon, flour and oats. Gradually add in whisked egg and stir until the dough starts to come together.

Place the dough on a well-floured surface. Knead the dough until smooth. Shape dough into a ball.

Bake at 350 degrees for 30 to 45 minutes or until golden brown. Makes 24 treats.

Spicy Yet Friendly Ginger Pops

Ingredients

1/4 cup pumpkin puree
(baked and seasoned
with turmeric and
ginger)
1 tablespoon ginger
infused water

Directions

Combine pumpkin puree and ginger infused water. Stir until smooth and pour into a pumpkin mold. Freeze for 2 hours. Makes 8 small pumpkin pops

Layers Pumpkin Frosty Bones

1/3 cup pumpkin puree
(baked and seasoned
with turmeric and
ginger)
1/3 cup yogurt

Using a bone ice tray mold, pour yogurt just to fill in the bottom of the bone mold. Freeze it for about an hour. Add pumpkin puree on top then another layer of yogurt . Freeze it for an hour before serving.

Strawberry Chips

Ingredients

5 large strawberries
1 tablespoon orange juice
1 teaspoon honey

Directions

In a blender, blend all the ingredients
Spread the liquid thinly on a baking mat.
Bake it at 250 degrees for 1 -1 1/2 hours.

Dip it on Banana Peanut Butter Dip

Pizza Friday

Ingredients

pizza dough
1/3 cup white rice flour
1/3 flour
1 teaspoon parsley
1 tablespoon coconut oil
1 egg

Topping

4 small tomatoes
1/2 teaspoon turmeric
1/2 cup shredded
cheddar mix cheese

Directions

In a bowl, combine all the dough ingredients. Place the dough on a well-floured surface. Knead the dough until smooth. Roll the dough to a 1/4-inch thickness and use a small round cookie cutter to make a round dough. Bake at 350 degrees for 20 minutes. Add the topping and bake it again for 10-15 minutes.

Soothing Banana Ginger Tea

Ingredients

1 ripe banana
1/2 teaspoon fresh grated ginger
2 1/2 cups of water

Directions

Cut off both ends of banana, and then cut in half. In a pot, combine the bananas, ginger and water. Boil for about 10 – 15 minutes. Turn off the heat. Put the lid on it and let it steep for 10 minutes. Strain the water and pour into a mug. Refrigerate overnight. Serve it with small frozen banana cubes.

Thanksgiving Leftovers

Ingredients

1/2 cup cooked turkey
(seasoned with turmeric)
1/3 cup steel oats
3 tablespoon pumpkin
puree
1/4 cup finely chopped
broccoli
1/3 cup shredded mix
cheddar cheese
1 egg

Directions

In a bowl, mix all the ingredients. On a baking sheet, teaspoon turkey mixture into dollops and bake it at 350 degrees for 5-10 minutes.

Apple Cinnamon Chips

Ingredients

4 large apples
cinnamon

Directions

Cut the apple in to slices (optional may include the skin). Spread the cut apples into a baking sheet and drizzle some cinnamon. Bake a 250 degrees for 1 or 1/2 hours.

Dip it on Pumpkin Ginger Honey Dip

Dips

Ingredients

Directions

Banana, Peanut Butter and Honey Dip

1 ripe banana
1/3 cup greek yogurt
1 teaspoon peanut butter
1/2 teaspoon honey

In a blender, blend 1/2 of ripe banana, yogurt, peanut butter and honey. Mash 1/2 of the banana and combine with the blended mixture.

Pumpkin and Ginger Honey Dip

1/2 cup pumpkin puree
(baked and seasoned
with turmeric and ginger)
2 tablespoon greek yogurt
1/2 teaspoon honey
black chia seeds

Fold in the pumpkin puree with the honey and greek yogurt. Drizzle some black chia seeds.

Author Bio

Rosalyn Acero

Rosalyn Acero is the founder and author of one of the most popular pet lifestyle blogs on the internet. Inspired by Sugar, her Golden Retriever, Rosalyn created Golden Woofs blog in October 2008 to share their life and dog-friendly adventures. With Sugar's happy smile and a love for photography, Golden Woofs quickly grew into a must-read blog for owners seeking information on all things dog. Her honest approach in writing about dog health, active living with a senior dog as well as sharing her creative, healthy dog-friendly recipes continues to bring readers back for more. Now with over 30,000 subscribers, combined blog and social media, Rosalyn has become the dog parent expert for easy homemade dog treats and general dog care.

CPSIA information can be obtained
at www.ICGtesting.com
Printed in the USA
BVOW10*1551140816
458872BV00003B/3/P

k's sympathies once tied him to the New Left. Indeed, in 1972, he
ke its language:

nay also see in the youth culture [of today] a profound starvation
denser family life, a richer life of the senses, the instincts, the mem-
No other group of young people in history was ever brought up
r a more intensive dose of value-free discourse, quantification, ana-
rationality, meritocratic competition, universal standards (IQ, Col-
Boards). What was almost wholly neglected in their upbringing was
oncrete, emotive, even tribal side of human nature. To that they
drawn in a desperate way, like air sucked into a vacuum. Music,
, sound, light, and feeling ran into the farthest extreme from indus-
suburban rationality.[40]

theless, *Unmeltable Ethnics* carried Novak on a course toward neocon-
n. For one thing, the moral-rationalist politics that he disdained he
cated in the reformist political tradition of America, shaped, he
l, by a puritanical, Yankee quest to make the world over, to purge it of
ave all reluctant souls. Reformers saw the world, he said, as so many
e parts, needing only to be retooled for more efficient coordination and
n. The reformers' democracy, he charged, was a "soulless" mass soci-
tituted by the quantifying process and norms of public opinion polls.
nic revolt, in turn, promised a new, more genuine democracy of "the
[41]

asingly in the 1970s, Novak came to identify the New Left itself as
tor of the WASP political tradition. And increasingly he denounced it
topianism, for its moral rigidness and self-righteousness, for its sense
iority and arrogance, and especially for its politics of guilt. Through-
decade Novak maintained his loyalties to the Democratic party, but
ning enthusiasm. After the debacle of 1972 he joined with other disaf-
emocrats to form the Committee for a Democratic Majority, commit-
noted, to retrieving the party from the New Class elites that had
t from its genuine constituencies.[42]

nspoken secret about *Unmeltable Ethnics* is just this: you did not have
e of the PIGS to identity with its thesis. *Unmeltable Ethnics* was an alle-
a changing America. Despite the precise nomenclature Novak
d, his book essentially portrayed a nation more and more divided
a rationalist culture controlled by a liberal elite, and the array of ordi-
ericans with their own quotidian hopes and ambitions. In 1978, in an
called "A Changed View," Novak described, on the one hand, the
ral cohort, born of affluent parents and products of elite universities,
rofessionals in law, education, and the media, zealous to change
by their progressive agenda. On the other hand, he described a com-
majority, the democratic majority, who drank beer and watched foot-

was so often quoted as saying: a neoconservative was a liberal who has been
mugged by reality.

If neoconservatives wished to give the public sector a little reality therapy,
the most discerning of them also expressed ambiguities about capitalism and
the free market economic system. Here, too, Kristol most effectively
described the problem. Like many neoconservatives Kristol endorsed capitalism, but not out of any genuine passion for it. He accepted capitalism because
it worked. Of all economic arrangements it most effectively answered human,
material wants. Socialism, one of the great and noble ideas in Western thinking, now lay in ruin, Kristol said. It remained the property only of utopians
and dictators, and those who just could not accept the democratic fact of a
market economy, where people vote with their pocketbooks.[33]

Why, then, Kristol's quarrel with capitalism? He wanted to distinguish
first between capitalism as an economic system and capitalism as a moral system. Capitalism, Kristol explained, orients individuals to the marketplace; it is
a system for the enhancement of material well-being. The bourgeois ethic (or
what historians sometimes call the "Protestant ethic") orients people toward
themselves; it is a means for regulating, or indeed moderating, the innate drives
of individuals toward pleasure, toward the enjoyment of those material acqui-
sitions that capitalism supplies abundantly. The capitalist ethic, said Kristol,
is an ethic of freedom; the bourgeois ethic is an ethic of control, of self-
discipline, above all of delayed gratifications. And it is the bourgeois ethic that
gives capitalism its legitimacy, he believed. It made capitalism something
more than a corollary of materialism or hedonism. For a long time this alliance
of the two ethics had worked well, he believed. Wealth and material success
roughly approximated the degree of personal virtue in those who amassed
them. Capitalism, Kristol wrote, "had a genuine relation to the individual as a
moral person. One acquired riches by being honest, diligent, prudent, pious,
and fortunate."[34]

But Kristol confronted a problem in this relationship, one anticipated by
economists such as Joseph Schumpeter and addressed with acuteness by
Daniel Bell in his 1974 book *The Cultural Contradictions of Capitalism*, previously considered. The problem was the estrangement of capitalism from the
moral system—the bourgeois ethic— that legitimated it. For capitalism, in its
material successes, created a climate in which the demand for the immediate
enjoyment of its fruits proved irresistible. The inner self-discipline that
marked the bourgeois personality, said Kristol, succumbed increasingly to a
culture, a capitalist culture, that forsook all self-discipline and yielded to an
imagination of indefinite material gratification. Parents who by hard work
and postponed pleasures gained affluence had a difficult time passing on their
good habits to their progeny, born into that affluence. Advertising, too, with
its message that anyone could purchase the necessities of a good life, conspired against this effort. To someone like Kristol who remembered the economic poverty of his Jewish youth, where, he said, to buy now and pay later

was a sign of personal weakness and moral turpitude, the contemporary credit culture of the United States signified national degeneration.[35]

In 1972, Kristol had become a regular contributor to the *Wall Street Journal*. But he showed no shyness in levying his moral censure against the very power brokers of American capitalism in his midst. For one of the culprits in America's declining public culture, Kristol insisted, was American business itself. Business, he lamented, knew no value except the bottom line. In the 1960s and 1970s, Kristol asserted, the contradictions of capitalism reached their absurd height when American business bought into the counterculture itself. It traded in the very commodities—books, records, movies, clothes— that were disseminating the antibusiness, antibourgeois culture of the Left. Those on the left, of course, called this process "co-optation." Kristol called it a sellout. Capitalism had arrived at the point where the singular measure of profit reigned; it could muster no moral or ideological resistance to the hedonistic, libertarian ethos of America.[36] Lenin once said that the rope on which he hung the capitalists would be one that he had bought from them.

Neoconservatism came into being as America experienced the transition to postindustrialism. Much of its political fury derived from the new sociological arrangements of that condition, especially the power shifts represented by the despised "New Class." But neoconservatism shared with other conservative expressions a restorative motif, an effort to abate, or undo, the sense of weightlessness, even of disintegration, in postindustrial conditions. Kristol longed for the solidarity of bourgeois society and its older values, however much he found bourgeois society "prosaic" and generally uninspiring, lacking in heroic virtues. But now he looked at a vulgar world of merely pecuniary values, a society morally adrift, anchorless. Other conservatives, as will be discussed, pursued the restorative effort along different lines. They wished to recover a sense of place, of community, of heritage; when all seemed to be yielding to liberalism's rationalism, they looked for kinship ties, for human relations blood-rich and thick, as their points of resistance.

When Michael Novak published his book *The Rise of the Unmeltable Ethnics* in 1972, he was completing a sojourn on the Left. *Unmeltable Ethnics* marked his mid-point in a transition to neoconservatism, and indeed by the end of the decade Novak had become the most prominent Catholic of that persuasion. Much of his writing to date had dealt with Church issues, but they often led to political translations that Novak himself carried into the radical politics of the sixties, including especially protests against the war in Vietnam. *Unmeltable Ethnics* reflects his career on the Left, but it also bears the markings of a conservative complaint now becoming familiar in the 1970s.

Novak subtitled his book *Politics and Culture in the Seventies*. In words that echoed the New Left, he began by describing an America beset by an oppressive political and moral culture, a rationalist strait-jacket that threatened to suffocate every genuine human passion and spontaneity. He saw American individualism become hollow and meaningless, depriving its citizens of the

---

bonds of fellowship, family, and tribal intimacy. intellectuals to show the way out, nor did he hail a tion. He looked instead to America's ethnic g dubbed the PIGS—the Poles, Italians, Greeks, and

The recent civil rights movement in the Unite Americas"—one black, one white; feminists desc one male, one female. Novak employed a similar d off the world of the Anglo-Saxon from the wor described two very different worlds.

The southern and eastern European immigrant to the United States a worldly sense that left ther ean rational and individualistic universe of the E pean groups. For the people whom Novak called t trait—an individualism that fed off the boundless American life and valued a material progress bo ambition. At the same time, however, the Anglo-S pulsion to control and order things, to impose dis nature, on public life, and on his own inner being. wrote Novak, the WASP sought to assert a moral bination of freedom and control, said Novak, gav special psychic character.[37]

Ethnic culture, by contrast, was blood-rich, thr of family and kinship ties. Ethnic consciousnes world the image of a new order or even of a soci no new moral universes, no politics of purification culture of earthiness, a naturalism accepting of the immigrant bearers of this culture—warm-heart into the cool, clean, controlled world of the Yank ern and eastern Europe," Novak wrote, "had to ness, cleanliness, reserve. They had to learn to n passion, to hold their hands still, to hold the mu find food and body odors offensive, to quieten th selves as coolly reasonable."[38]

Anglo-Saxonism, said Novak, secured its g through its control of the corporate headquarter tem. But Novak also highlighted another elite. Ch *nics* has the title "The Intellectuals of the Northea cially in the elite eastern universities, Novak Enlightenment, the cult of reason and skepticism the traditional values and the habits of ordinary growing hostility toward such people and towar Vice President Agnew (Spiro Theodore Anagnos grant) lashed out against the student radicals (" snobs"), Novak believed he saw an old culture wa

ball games on television. They were, withal, the better hopes of American democracy.[43]

Historian and sociologist Robert Nisbet also spoke for the recovery of community. Born in Los Angeles in 1913, Nisbet enjoyed an academic career that took him from Berkeley to Columbia and won him many honors for scholarship, including the prestigious Jefferson lectureship in 1988. He published his first book, *The Quest for Community*, in 1953 and thereafter joined his studies to a self-conscious articulation of conservative principles. Nisbet's book *The Twilight of Authority*, a major conservative offering of the 1970s, made a pointed critique of American society. As much as any other conservative in this decade, Nisbet embodied a kind of European conservatism, one that defended the idea of an organic society and faulted the excesses of individualism. If he did not accept the metaphysically rooted conservatism of older conservatives, he shared their ideals of tradition and continuity and their respect for institutions.

In a 1978 essay, Nisbet attempted to summarize conservatism by listing several key values. He cited first the indispensability of religion and a sensitivity to the sacred, and added the need for family, the importance of social rank, the imperative right of property, the significance of local community and region, and the decentralization and diffusion of political power. But one item in the list particularly prevailed in Nisbet's sociology and social advocacy—the necessity of what he called "intermediate" groups and organizations.[44] By intermediate Nisbet meant communities of participation—fraternal, religious, ethnic, and social clubs, PTAs and neighborhood action groups, labor unions and local governments—that stand between the individual citizen and the state. When he wrote his book *Prejudices* in 1982 and filled in the entry for "conservatism," Nisbet summarized its core value. "The essence of this body of ideas," he wrote, "is the protection of the social order—family, neighborhood, local community, and region foremost—from the ravishments of the centralized political state."[45] And in *Twilight of Authority* he warned that "the gradual disappearance of all the intermediate institutions" that had been staples of Western society now threatened to make democracy itself "a new science of despotism."[46]

Nisbet described as a central theme in Western civilization the struggle between those forces that sustained intermediate societies and those that eroded them. In the United States, that struggle had become particularly acute, given the special circumstances of its history. For among those forces that conspired against the intermediate societies and their social function were the ideologies of individualism, those value systems that celebrated the unique character of each person and gave high priority to the autonomous freedom of each individual. But an equal threat came from another source: the state. Although Americans deluded themselves that their democracy had liberated them from the tyranny of monarchical forms of government, or spared them the horrors of recent totalitarianism, Nisbet warned that liberal democracy was not immune from the controlling nemesis of state power.

Modern liberalism, Nisbet described, began with the Enlightenment and the French Revolution. From the first it inherited the passion to standardize and rationalize all human relationships. Enlightenment savants, Nisbet said, disdained local and traditional arrangements as archaic, the accidents of history, and unprogressive tribal enclaves. The French Revolution, in turn, generated massive bureaucracy, the "fourth branch of government," as Nisbet labeled it. Bureaucracy stifled society's vitality; it vitiated intermediate societies as its passion for uniformity progressively superseded the discretionary practices of those groups. Contemporary America, Nisbet noted, had become a litigious society. The minutia of law superseded traditional social patterns as the determinants of personal relationships. The compulsion to compel uniformity through the activity of the state, Nisbet warned, had brought the United States, crucial differences notwithstanding, to a likeness with the totalitarian states of the twentieth century.[47]

Democratic society, Nisbet believed, experiences both the tendency to control and the tendency to liberate. He saw the United States moving in the direction of wider tolerance of individual choice in manners and morals, and extending First Amendment freedoms beyond any limits recognizable to previous generations. But Nisbet also described, and lamented, a prevailing culture of subjectivity, as witness the youth rebellion and counterculture of the 1960s. Such an evolution, he believed, derived in part from erroneous notions of individuality and personhood, notions shared by libertarian conservatives and liberals alike. Liberal societies tend to see the individual as an autonomous unit, a self-contained reality. That view may appear paradoxical, given the proclivity to collectivize that Nisbet also described. But in fact, one tendency reinforced the other. The more intensely people experienced the anomie of modern life, said Nisbet, the more acutely felt became the need to create a semblance of unity, of belonging, of oneness with the whole. Hence, then, the rationale of the modern democratic state. But government, Nisbet said, could not safely substitute for "society." Nisbet saw no easy way out of this dilemma, save to emphasize a recovery of natural communities and the preservation of local and organic organizations opposed to the synthetic and oppressive unity fashioned by the leviathan state.[48]

George Will, on the other hand, could have written an essay on the conservative appreciation of the state. In Will we have another conservative response to the America of the 1970s. Will had much in common with the neoconservatives and their complaints about the new liberalism, especially its preoccupation with an equality of results forged through government social programs. He shared with Novak and Nisbet a quest for meaningful community, for substance, and for common identity amid the centrifugal forces of postindustrial America. But Will insisted, in contrast to most other conservatives, that government had a role to play in redirecting American life. He called himself a "Tory conservative" when he defended that role.

Will was born in Champaign, Illinois in 1941, the son of a philosophy professor. He pursued his academic studies through a doctorate degree in political science at Princeton, but opted for journalism over teaching. His political commentary, marked by its elegant prose and wit, made him a forceful conservative partisan in the 1970s and won him a Pulitzer Prize in 1977. Later, his Sunday morning appearances on the David Brinkley program gave him an expanded national audience.

Will liked to say that he argued for a particularly "European" kind of conservatism, one that, regrettably, too few self-styled American conservatives appreciated. He traced his philosophical pedigree to Edmund Burke, John Henry Newman, and Benjamin Disraeli, but it also linked him to a traditionalist conservative mind in the United States as represented by individuals such as Ralph Adams Cram, Irving Babbitt, Paul Elmer More, Peter Viereck, and Russell Kirk. This conservatism exercises a particular imagination—a respect for the past, a feel for antiquity, a respect for the fragile character of civilization, a skepticism about human nature and attempts to perfect human society. Will and his conservative predecessors felt acutely the forces of disorder and social disintegration. They looked for the stabilizing influences of time and place. It was not enough, Will said, for conservatives simply to celebrate liberty and freedom or to look to the marketplace to arbitrate social needs. Conservatism must know and cultivate the preserving connections that joined past to present. It must embody a mystique of history, of time and place. To this extent, Will faulted the neoconservatives. "They do not have stained-glass minds," he said.[49]

Will's views struck many as elitist and aristocratic. They were. But Will quite happily stepped outside the Gothic church to walk among the people in the streets. For at the heart of Will's conservatism there flourished a certain democratic enthusiasm and a respect for the decent civilization wrought by ordinary Americans. In his historical reflections Will showed more respect for the achievements of plain people in sod houses on the prairie than for the bewigged authors of the Constitution. American civilization, he wrote, grew from "the routine mud of common experience, and its accomplishments were more than a little heroic."[50]

Will wanted his conservatism to be, in the tradition of Burke, a conservatism of place. Its democratic quality derived from that concern. Will could write appreciatively of much maligned, old, industrial cities like Cleveland. He could thrill to the enthusiasms of Nebraskans for the football accomplishments of their Cornhuskers. Even the mass hysteria of a Bruce Springsteen rock concert gained his appreciation. Little League games in small Maryland towns also attracted his editorial observations, and his pen (and Will wrote everything with a black, gilt-edged ink pen) could rise to poetic expression as he watched his beloved Chicago Cubs baseball team.[51]

But Will also witnessed the inroads of another America—the fashionable and trendy ways of the new upper middle class, what the pundits began to label in the early 1980s the "Yuppies." Will had worked for a while in Colorado and had seen the Colorado of the Old West, the mining camps and the wheat fields. Now he saw a Colorado of inrushing eastern skiers and the Hollywood jetset. Now the state flourished with chic boutiques and condominiums. Will recoiled from all the trappings of the newly affluent—the butcherblock kitchens, the pasta makers, the Nautilus exercise machines, the stress-management courses, the cordless phones. America, he feared, was changing from a nation of authentic communities to one of consumer groupings in which the thin and random associations of lifestyle similarities replaced the bonds of memory and place. What resulted, Will feared, was a desolate and soulless inner life in America's comfortable quarters.[52]

In many of his essays, Will showed a concern for the erosions in America that rendered it disparate and dangerously divisive. Its public life failed to generate or express a shared culture or value system. The United States, he feared, lacked a meaningful and cohesive core of identity. He described a proliferation of interest groups each of which looked to the national government to support its special needs. The state, consequently, no longer symbolized the higher republican ethic of the nation; it resembled more a public trough, from which each faction and interest felt entitled to swill. Daniel Bell, it was noted earlier, had warned that such a habit would be a norm of postindustrial politics. Will faulted both liberalism, which he believed had created what G. K. Chesterton had labeled the servile state, and conservatism, with its hardened philosophies of laissez-faire economics. Will, in fact, incurred the scorn of both liberals and conservatives when he opined quite bluntly that the United States simply tolerated too many liberties—for abortion, for pornography, for hate speech, for businesses wishing to trade with communist nations, for exemptions from military service, and in general for discretionary flaunting of established moral norms. The nation had arrived at a condition, he believed, where wants had become confused with rights, and to secure a want, one had only to proclaim it as a "right."[53]

Will's concern for preserving the cohesive bonds of society led him to specify a particular kind of conservatism. He identified as his models Bismarck and Disraeli, pioneers of the welfare state, and Will himself honored the achievements of the New Deal in establishing a protective Social Security system. Such social programs, Will believed, reflected an authentic conservative interest in the material well-being of all people who constitute themselves a nation. Without a minimum of material security, he warned, a society becomes fractured by alienated, uprooted, and angry elements. The order that society needs may then find its answer only in a brutal totalitarianism that absorbs all freedoms.[54]

Will's celebrations of localist America and his endorsement of the welfare state did not exclude a genuine aristocratic quality in his conservatism. He acknowledged the value of social rank and moral influence, and he wanted government to reflect them. Will could praise the examples of European monarchies or the aristocratic personage of a Winston Churchill, but his conservatism also had American roots in the Whig political culture of the nineteenth century and its model of the moral state. Will did not want American government to be merely prosaic or utilitarian. It should inspire and not merely copy the democratic norms of American life, he believed. But, in 1977, when Queen Elizabeth in England was celebrating her Silver Jubilee amid regal splendor and public rejoicing, President Jimmy Carter, Will regretfully reported, was going before national television wearing a sweater.[55] Nor was Will pleased when a television program showed President Gerald Ford buttering his own English muffins in the White House kitchen.[56] Ever ready to lecture his readers on the higher, symbolic uses of government, Will concluded with regret that "the modern servile state possesses, at most, utility, never dignity."[57]

Amidst the amorphousness and intangibility of postindustrial life, Will pursued a conservative quest for the recovery of place and belonging. But he would not permit an indiscriminate democracy, with its disdain for form, to be the vehicle of that effort. That inclination had prevented American government, in contrast to its European counterparts, from providing its people with the symbols, the pageantry, and the historical emblems that furnish a common imagination and an inspiration for a nation. Will wished, in essence, to inscribe aristocratic forms into democratic society, not to diminish democracy, but to ennoble it, to imbue it with substance and concreteness. Democracy, Will insisted, needs a precious combination of the common and the superior. It needs leadership that conveys not just power but eminence, influence, and moral example. Leadership is unworthy of the title if it does not stand out from mass tastes and even mass opinion.[58] The conservative Peter Viereck once wrote that "democracy is the best government on earth when it tries to make all its citizens aristocrats."[59] Will shared that conviction.

The conservative movement of the 1970s, politically and intellectually, grew inevitably from the reaction against the excesses of the 1960s and to that extent coincided with the normal cycle in American politics. But we must not overlook the special content of 1970s conservatism that gives it historical significance in its own right. For both in the changes that effected a significant shift in the major political parties and in the rhetorical style and symbolism used by conservative writers, the movement had a clear temporal location. It could draw on the traditionalism and the moral suasion of an established conservative literature, but in applying these devices, it had its eyes on the decisive shifts that were redefining America in the 1970s.

Postindustrialism, as we have seen, had its uprooting effects. From neighborhood to corporation, the social structures that once provided a modicum of definition—location, work, stable and predictable human interconnections—now lost their ability to provide individuals with a sense of stability and familiarity. These changes, as E. J. Dionne, Jr., has noted, greatly affected American politics. He described the change this way:

The party system of the New Deal era was relatively stable because definable groups voted together and largely held together, even in bad times. Now, almost everything conspires against group solidarity. Unions are in trouble, and conservatives have done everything they could to weaken them. The new jobs in the service industry promote individualism. The decline of the small towns and the old ethnic enclaves and the rise of new suburbs, exurbs, and condominium developments further weakens social solidarity. Old urban neighborhoods feel abandoned by the liberal politicians whom they once counted on for support.[60]

As a politics of solidarity weakened, a politics of abstract national groups became more pronounced. Increasingly into the 1980s politics gained whatever concreteness it could by reifying general descriptive characteristics and turning them into special interests that brought their own demands to government. Thus "women," "blacks," "gays," or the "disabled," stood for special, often "victimized" constituencies with their proxy-holders in the legislatures. Conservatives seized on the transition and made capital by reinvoking the "real" people, the broader democratic constituencies, and they tried to restore some wholeness to the fractured America on which they gazed. In the middle 1980s and beyond, liberals, too, embraced the restorative theme as a needed corrective for American life and politics.[61]

In a postindustrial age, communications becomes decisive. As Dionne also observes, American politics by the late 1980s had moved from message to symbolism, or a politics in which the symbol was the message. Thus, the furlough of a convicted killer, Willie Horton, by the Governor of Massachusetts, Michael Dukakis, emerged as a major campaign issue by George Bush when he and Dukakis vied for the presidency in 1988. Horton was not an empty symbol by any means, not in crime-ridden America. Nor was symbolism as a television tool for politics new (recall the little girl counting down the daisy petals to a nuclear bomb ignition in 1964). Symbolism, however, constitutes an intellectual short-cut. Conservatives in the 1970s and 1980s gained in persuasion because they did seize on the changes in America and often addressed them meaningfully. But they were also given to intellectual short-cutting. In an era of declining substance, people seek new solidarities; or they invent them. Hence the temptation to reify, to create monolithic entities from multiplicate complexities. Such expressions as "the real people," or "PIGS," or "secular humanism," or "New Class" gave misplaced concreteness to these complexities. Intellectual conservatism, with its traditional respect for the real and the concrete, would surely gain by respect for those qualities in its persuasive endeavors.

nine

On Liberalism

The 1970s forced on American liberalism a crisis of identity and definition. It had emerged from the 1960s already badly shaken, with the most serious challenge posed by a New Left that wanted badly to disassociate itself from this, the acknowledged political norm of American history. The New Left questioned everything that, in its eyes, rendered liberalism a reactionary presence in American life. Liberalism, it believed, had long lost, if it had ever possessed, the ideological resolve or the institutional power to be truly revolutionary. That challenge, of course, had already pushed many who called themselves liberals into a more emphatic leftist position, one that left liberalism badly divided in the 1970s. But by the end of the decade, the resurgent conservatism we have observed was taking moderate liberals into the neoconservative camp. Democrats running for political office in 1976 often shunned the liberal label altogether.

In 1976 the neoconservative publication *Commentary* held a symposium to which several dozen intellectuals contributed, addressing the questions "What is a Liberal—Who is a Conservative?" The intellectual surgery undertaken produced some compelling suggestions about the current course of American politics and the intellectual shifts that attended its changing scene. If many contended that the terms "liberal" and "conservative" had lost all usefulness, they nonetheless offered insights as to how we had arrived at such a state of confusion and uncertainty about America's political direction. For none seemed to doubt that in the United States of the 1970s, uncertainty was king.

Clearly, some specific issues and events had upset the usual political and ideological alignments. At the outset of the decade, the Vietnam War still raged. Then the American bombing in Cambodia brought violent campus reactions, denoted especially by the deaths of students at Kent State University and the bombing at the University of Wisconsin. Opposition to the war had already taken American liberals out of alliance with Democratic foreign policies in the Kennedy and Johnson years. Some could give at least tentative credence to the New Left charge that America had always been an imperialist nation, its inherent racism now implicating the country in a violent and inhumane war against progressive Third World forces. But opposition to Vietnam did not of itself nullify one's liberal affiliation. Many liberals defended the Democratic party's long-standing internationalism that they believed had defended freedom in two world wars and in the struggle against Soviet totalitarianism. They wanted America to preserve its activist posture in the world. Against this commitment, Democratic presidential candidate George McGovern in 1972 called for more than American disengagement from Vietnam; he wanted an end to "cold war paranoia," too.[1] In reaction, internationalist-minded Democrats like Jeane Kirkpatrick and Irving Kristol drifted into the neoconservative camp and sometimes into alliance with the Republican party.

That tendency became more visible when compounded by another foreign policy issue—Israel. The radical Left in America had become strongly critical of the Jewish state, supported to the hilt by American money, and standing defiant as it faced rival Arab nations, whom the radicals associated sympathetically with the Third World. That perspective had majority support in the United Nations, which at one point equated Zionism with racism. The new isolationist mood in liberalism clearly threatened to weaken American commitment to Israel, as American Jews readily perceived. Many Jews who opposed the American presence in Vietnam insisted on United States commitment to what they saw as a beleaguered Israel.[2]

Among issues at home, race and racial politics created serious strains in liberalism. However slow and even begrudging at first, liberal support for the civil rights movement became overwhelming in the 1960s and helped give liberalism its major post-New Deal cause. But it also became clear that the black movement would sorely test liberal principles. The busing issue was the first step toward what many began to describe as a liberalism based on statistical equality, a countinghouse liberalism that satisfied its progressive intentions when it could point to numbers that suggested an equality of results. Affirmative Action programs brought a similar disaffection that enhanced the neoconservative movement. In New York City an open admissions program, designed to create a greater representation of poor, urban blacks, induced open dissent by academics and others. They saw not only a betrayal of standards but a threat to a particular tradition of higher learning. These directives caused liberals such as historian Eric Goldman to wonder whether this new politics took liberalism altogether away from its historic commitments. They appeared, he said, to "cut counter" to the traditional liberal focus on equal opportunity as opposed to a "forced egalitarianism." The new centrality of race and gender in America, in short, was imposing on liberalism a new methodology designed to repair the past. But it possibly created strains that liberalism could not bear.[3]

This stress point in American liberalism forced a painful response among American Jews. Black-Jewish tensions became a focus of concern. Not surprisingly, then, it was the neoconservative Jewish *Commentary* that undertook the vast symposium on liberalism.

The 1960s bequeathed to liberalism yet another divisive matter. In a way that anticipated a major shift in American politics in the last decades of the twentieth century, the radical movement of the 1960s began to make "culture," often meaning nothing more complicated than "lifestyle," a matter of political contention. Culture, though, as a political issue, carried a lot of baggage. It included environmentalism, a priority that often signalled a lesser commitment to economic growth and otherwise celebrated a down-sized pattern of living. Culture also included matters of personal discretion, as in the taking of drugs or smoking of marijuana. These expressions of the counterculture tested liberalism's long-standing tolerance of individual choice. The Freudian strain in the New Left and its celebration of sexual liberation also caused discomfort for many middle-class liberals. Something as simple as hairstyle came to embody large political symbolism. If liberalism opened to the new culture, it did so at considerable political cost. Among American working-class families, with their traditional ways of living, with their stake in an expanding economy, and with their religion and patriotism, the counterculture represented a direct frontal assault.[4] Merle Haggard, the country music star, immortalized the socio-cultural clash in his popular song of 1971, "Okie from Muskogee."

Why had liberalism come to such an impasse and to such a splintering in its ranks? Some analysts tried to gain historical perspective on the dilemma. It made sense to look at liberalism in the nineteenth century when it pursued an economic system open to new initiatives and freed from historic constraints posed by government. Government did well, liberalism believed, when it functioned to remove institutional impediments, including its own, against the natural forces of man and nature. Liberalism's faith taught that out of such a pursuit greater wealth and fairer distribution would result. In the United States in the late nineteenth century, the liberal program turned against the trusts and their constraining power. This faith held until the New Deal confronted the Great Depression of the 1930s. Liberals now concluded that merely removing restrictions did not assure the results expected and that government must have a role both in creating opportunities and in assuring minimal degrees of economic security for its citizens. To many liberals in the 1970s these New Deal axioms continued to underscore their philosophy of government. They took exception, however, when a more aggressive liberalism began to emerge, one that now insisted that government must do more than guarantee equality of opportunity; it must strive to assure a proximate equality of results.[5]

The most interesting issue in liberalism's intramural debate concerned just this problem—the problem of freedom versus equality. It was observed that whereas conservative theory tries to balance the values of tradition and social continuity with individual liberty, liberalism tries to balance the values of liberty and equality.[6] Joseph Epstein, editor of *The American Scholar,* remarked: "Take nearly any important question of our day and there you will find the liberal spread-eagle by his indecision over choosing between the different (and as often as not, contradictory) objectives of liberty and equality."[7]

Those who clearly gave the greater priority to liberty as opposed to equality often found themselves moving away from liberal politics and into neoconservatism. They believed that the liberal program had substituted categories of race and gender—as in busing or affirmative action—for the notion of the autonomous individual. Midge Decter insisted, therefore, that liberalism's great, revolutionary contribution to Western history was the idea that each individual "is, and is entitled to be treated as, an irreducible individual." "What it means," she added, "is that no person may be forcibly imprisoned within the class or clan or even family into which he was born."[8] Sidney Hook reinforced these ideas. Hook, a prominent Marxist philosopher in the 1930s, later followed a career from liberalism to neoconservatism, a trajectory common among the New York intellectuals. By Hook's account, individual freedom, whether "negative" freedom from arbitrary restraints, or "positive" freedom through greater access to social and economic opportunity, defined liberalism's core principle. "In both cases," Hook added, "it was the individual person who was to be liberated regardless of the number and character of his or her social ties, origins, or relations. . . . The liberal, therefore, professed to be blind to color, deaf to religious dogma, indifferent to sex and national origin." When liberalism turned to assuring an equality of representation by sex and race, Hook believed it betrayed its principles. He further lamented the "bureaucratic despotism" that had emerged to enforce that equality.[9] To Irving Kristol, "liberalism . . . has become far more interested in equality than in liberty."[10]

Issues of freedom and equality spoke directly to major social and political questions before Americans in the 1970s. They were thus inseparable from discussions about admissions into colleges and professional schools, about hiring in academic departments, government bureaucracies, and fire and police departments, and about the assignment of children to their schools and the transportation arrangements needed to get them there. All these agitated issues and the public discourse surrounding them might gain from serious intellectual analysis. The 1970s, in fact, produced two significant contributions to the political theory of these two American principles. Given the political context in which they appeared, it was not remarkable that they won such attention and acclaim.

In 1971, John Rawls published a magisterial work. *A Theory of Justice* returned to philosophizing in the grand tradition. He offered a book full of logical disputation, a speculative treatise in the manner of the great metaphysicians, as stimulating as it was challenging. By its very nature the book surprised; in the era of analytical philosophy some expected never to see such an undertaking again. Furthermore, Rawls seemed to show the way to the needed recovery for liberalism's intellectual malaise. His book made an immediate impact. Extensive commentary greeted the publication, and within four years a substantial book of essays, fourteen in all, offered lengthy critical assessments.[11]

Rawls wanted to establish a contemporary theory of liberalism. To do so, he believed he must address liberalism's two root traditions—the utilitarian and the intuitionist. "My guiding aim," he wrote, "is to work out a theory of justice that is a viable alternative to these doctrines which have long dominated our philosophical tradition."[12] But he gave more attention to utilitarianism because he judged it the dominant influence in the West. Specifically, Rawls had in mind such major works as Shaftesbury's *An Inquiry Concerning Virtue and Merit* (1711), Francis Hutcheson's *An Inquiry Concerning Moral Good and Evil* (1725), David Hume's *A Treatise on Human Nature* (1751), Adam Smith's *A Theory of the Moral Sentiments* (1759), Jeremy Bentham's *The Principles of Morals and Legislation* (1789), John Stuart Mill's *Utilitarianism* (1863), and Henry Sidgwick's *The Methods of Ethics* (1907).[13] To these, Rawls formulated his own 587-page reply.

By classical utilitarianism, Rawls meant the idea that a society is rightly ordered, and therefore just, when it is arranged so as to achieve the greatest net balance of satisfaction as measured through all of the individuals belonging to it. Often utilitarianism argued that as an individual acts by way of calculating his advantages and satisfactions, so, too, should the society as a whole. Society's goal is simply to advance the welfare of the group. Rawls saw in utilitarianism a radical shift toward the priority of society in ethical reasoning. Efficient administration and social cooperation, always with the end of achieving the greatest *net* balance of satisfaction, now defined utilitarian ends.[14]

Before outlining his major reservations about utilitarianism, Rawls announced that he intended to argue for a rival concept, "justice as fairness." Furthermore, he placed his methodological defense of that concept on an ancient philosophical device, the contractual theory of society. Rawls wrote with Locke, Rousseau, and Kant in mind, positing, like them and others, an original, presocietal condition of individuals, and speculating with them on what terms a society, or a collective of some kind, should emerge from such a group and how it might justify its continued existence. "Men are to decide in advance," wrote Rawls, "how they are to regulate their claims against one another and what is to be the foundation charter of their society."[15]

Rawls elaborated his contractual theory by describing what became his much-discussed "original position." Justice as fairness, he argued, must emerge from a basic precondition, a hypothetical situation, but one necessary to settle in advance under what terms individuals will agree to establish and perpetuate social arrangements. Rawls insisted, therefore, that in speculating about the original position, and agreeing to live by its specifications, none knows his place in society—not his class position or his social status. Neither does she know her natural assets or abilities, strength or intelligence. Each individual considers the founding principles of justice, the original social contract, under this "veil of ignorance." "This ensures," said Rawls, "that no one is advantaged or disadvantaged in the choice of principles by the outcome of natural chance or the contingency of social circumstances. Since all are similarly situated and no one is able to design principles to favor his particular condition, the principles of justice are the result of a fair agreement or bargain." Rawls assumed in individuals both a rational and a moral nature. That assumption enabled the concept of justice as fairness.[16]

Rawls' system valued liberty. In justice as fairness, persons accept in advance a principle of equal liberty. Utilitarians, Rawls acknowledged, valued liberty, but only because they judged a free society to be conducive to greater happiness, on balance, for the whole than a non-free society. Rawls considered justice as fairness superior to utilitarianism in giving no claim to anyone who took pleasure in the lesser liberty of another. Rawls believed that utilitarianism erred seriously in failing, in its calculation of satisfactions, to note from what those satisfactions derive. Rawls could thus reply: "The pleasure [one] takes in other's [sic] deprivations is wrong in itself: it is a satisfaction which requires the violation of a principle to which he would agree in the original position." No one, that is, would agree to such a contraction of liberty since none, in the veil of ignorance, could assume that he or she would not be among the deprived. For emphasis, Rawls added summarily that in justice as fairness the concept of right is prior to that of good.[17]

What, then, constituted the actual principles of justice? Here are Rawls' formulations:

> First: each person is to have an equal right to the most extensive basic liberty compatible with a similar liberty for others.
> Second: social and economic inequalities are to be arranged so that they are both (a) reasonably expected to be to everyone's advantage, and (b) attached to positions and offices open to all.

These principles, Rawls maintained, must govern the assignment of rights and duties and regulate the distribution of social and economic advantages. Rawls also assigned a serial order to these principles; the first had priority over the second. Liberties and economic gains were not exchangeable.[18]

But the second principle, as one might expect, became the more controversial. In defending it, Rawls touched on the particular factors that defined the newer kind of liberalism he wanted to advance. Clearly, he did not want liberalism to move in the direction of an absolute social equality; nor was *A Theory of Justice* an anticapitalist manifesto. Economic differences may be quite legitimate and necessary, he believed. But these differences can have legitimacy only if it can be shown that they do not exist at the expense of an actual or expected loss of economic status to the least advantaged in society. "The intuitive idea is that the social order is not to establish and secure the more attractive prospects of those better off unless doing so is to the advantage of those less fortunate." As a corollary, Rawls wrote that an inequality in expectation is permissible if reducing that inequalty would make the working class even more worse off. The greater expectations allowed to entrepreneurs, Rawls urged, should encourage them to act in a manner that raises the long-term expectations of laboring classes as well as their own.[19] To contrast with utilitarianism, Rawls insisted that one may not justify differences in income or organizational powers by saying that the disadvantages that accrue to one group weigh less, in sum, than the advantages that accrue to another.[20]

Rawls believed he had identified principles under which individuals would agree to establish a society and under which they would have no cause not to abide by its rules. Although he began with the hypothetical original position, he moved later in his book to specific points that followed from the principles of justice as fairness. Thus, Rawls acknowledged that demands of public order and security might require the government to act in restricting some liberties, but it ought not, usually, to restrict even intolerant groups who would appear to threaten liberty. Freedom of conscience must prevail to the highest degree possible.[21]

On other matters, Rawls defended constitutional democracy, based on full participation by citizens in the political process. Liberty requires checks on the powers of the legislature, he believed, and he relied on the traditional checks and balances within the constitutional system to uphold personal liberty and restrict power. Rawls himself did not believe that justice as fairness mandated either capitalism or socialism. He insisted only that fairness, as opposed to formal equality, requires a specific role for government. It must assure equal opportunities in education and culture, police the power of business, and assure a minimum income by any number of distributive devices. As one commentator said, "Although Rawls does not put it in these terms, it looks as if economic justice is given institutional expression by the organs of a welfare state."[22]

Respondents to Rawls often found it difficult to quarrel with the benign principles of his theory. He laid it on foundations that seemed uncontroversial and he gave it an application that made liberalism conform to ideals of fairness, protection of the weak, and withal, individualism and even competitiveness in the market place. Clearly, liberalism gained from Rawls a needed theoretical revitalization. All the more instructive, then, was the reaction against him. It came vigorously from the Left and the Right.

Milton Fisk, a Marxist professor, provided a criticism from that perspective. Fisk saw in Rawls a formidable if nonetheless dangerous fortification of liberal democracy on precisely those terms by which an ideology of freedom had become, historically, the prop of bourgeois capitalism. Rawls' powerful deception, Fisk tried to show, lay in his ability to persuade that the conditions of the original position were inherently neutral and also expressive of our essential human nature. In that way he established their immediate intellectual priority. For Fisk, a key passage in Rawls linked his system to Kant. Rawls wrote: "My suggestion is that we think of the original position as the point of view from which noumenal selves see the world. The parties qua noumenal selves have complete freedom to choose whatever principles they wish; but they also have a desire to express their nature as rational and equal members of the intelligible realm with precisely this liberty to choose, that is, as beings who can look at the world in this way and express this perspective in their life as members of society."[23]

This liberal notion, Fisk believed, ignores the true nature of thought and the derivation of governing principles in human society. The thoughts that one takes an interest in defending, said Fisk, rarely emerge from disinterested contemplation. "They are not one's own mental productions from one's own raw experiential materials." Rather, said Fisk, these principles of religion, morality, and philosophy signify the inculcating power of dominant institutions and an apparatus of offices and individuals with an interest in strengthening them. For the Marxist, the Rawlsian system represented a familiar if nonetheless dangerous paradox: the natural or normative freedom Rawls so carefully establishes eventuates in the historic conditions of bourgeois-capitalist society. Dominant groups always manipulate thought, but the capitalist hegemony has the more effectively maintained its control by contriving the criteria of its own acceptance. In this case, the beguiling devices of the original position—its foundation in neutrality, freedom, reason, and morality—enhance bourgeois credibility. They do so because these normative values obscure its power interests. "In short," wrote Fisk, "liberal freedom of thought provides a cover for the hidden persuaders that aid oppressing groups."[24] Rawls' treatise to this extent confirmed modern Marxist suspicions of a universalist and normative value system hiding behind bourgeois power.

Also for Fisk, Rawls' contractual system began with autonomous individuals and could end only in a market economy based in competitive individualism and all its attending consequences. Rawls, said Fisk, could derive from his founding principles only an anemic and essentially meaningless ideal of community and could ignore the dominant role played by class in the social constructions of power. Whereas the earlier Lockean contract served to dismantle the whole apparatus of feudalism and prepare for a free, market economy, Rawls' contract, Fisk urged, was defensive, essentially "conservative." It suited the 1970s, he argued. Rawls offered a constructive criticism that could urge reform but not a dismantling of the capitalist system. It served thereby to give capitalism the renewal of life it needed in the face of a rising skepticism. Rawls showed to its detractors that capitalism could address the oppression and injustice that its challengers believed to be inherent in it. But to Fisk that strategy merely condemned Rawlsian liberalism the more. It merely shows, he said, "that the imagination of liberal critics does not extend beyond conserving the market and liberal democracy."[25]

From a conservative perspective, University of Chicago professor Allan Bloom also maintained that *A Theory of Justice* did not do enough. (Bloom's critique assumes an added interest because he became the author of a conservative manifesto in 1987, *The Closing of the American Mind,* a best-selling book.) Bloom conceded that liberal democracy needed an intellectual defense. It had not, in his judgment, produced in the twentieth century an apologist to match the destructive toll taken by thinkers like Marx and Nietzsche in the nineteenth. And in the century of Hitler and Stalin, he said, one would have to do more than make some corrections in utilitarianism to pull it off.[26] He believed, however, that Rawls did not supply the want.

Bloom saw in Rawls a traditional concern with individual liberties, but one modified by a new ethical measure. For Rawls' new liberalism was clearly more egalitarian that its predecessor models. All should be equal, Bloom paraphrased Rawls, but if inequalities exist they must be suffered to do so by the permission of the least advantaged members of society. Every gain made at the top must find legitimation by expanded attentiveness to the well-being of those below. Thus Rawls's innovation, Bloom said, "is to incorporate the maxims of contemporary social welfare into the fundamental principles of political justice." Government need not ask whether such recipients have mixed their labor with these awards, nor does it ask, with Marx, whether these awards correspond to individual needs.[27]

Bloom, a student of philosopher Leo Strauss, registered reactions against Rawls that reflect Old Right conservative (as opposed to neoconservative) judgments. He found Rawls' new liberal democracy unheroic and ignoble. Its obsession with equality, its appeal to a lowest common denominator for a measure of fairness, its indiscriminate interest in the self-worth of all individuals left Bloom in aesthetic retreat from so banal a society. Bloom contrasted Rawls with Tocqueville. An enthusiast for democracy, Tocqueville nevertheless feared that democracy took its toll on intellectual and moral superiority, that its levelling tendencies posed the greatest threats to democracy's wellbeing. Neither the danger implicit in the tyranny of the majority, nor the blandishments of modern mass society, Bloom feared, seemed to trouble Rawls. Bloom saw in the new liberal democracy a happiness-driven society— not a noble one. He saw in it a great collectivity, but little space for bold and spirited individuals. He saw in it little room for sacrifice or risk, but lots of room for self-satisfaction.[28]

A Theory of Justice gave liberalism an intellectual boost. Discussion of the book seemed to legitimate the role of the state in influencing a greater measure of equality in American society and there was no want of suggestions as to how that goal might be achieved. Nonetheless, Rawls' book appeared also at a time of conservative insurgency. Neoconservatives and others questioned the effectiveness of the Great Society programs and the social "experimenta-tion" undertaken by liberal politicians. In fact, some undertook to challenge the legitimacy of the state altogether. The 1970s saw a renewal of libertarian-ism among the reigning political ideologies and economic theories. Milton Friedman, who had made a career reorienting Keynesian macroeconomics and restoring the credibility of laissez-faire liberalism, won the Nobel Prize in economics in 1976. Libertarian ideology attained enough of a following by 1972 to organize a Libertarian political party with professor John Hospers as its presidential candidate. But the libertarian renewal also owed something to Robert Nozick, who published in 1974 his manifesto *Anarchy, State, and Utopia*, a National Book Award winner.

Libertarianism redefines liberalism in terms of its classical roots in the eighteenth century. It is a doctrine of the minimal state. From its earlier for-mulations in individuals like Adam Smith and Thomas Jefferson, libertarian-ism variously championed free market economics and celebrated the priority of the individual over the collectivity in matters of morality and law. In the United States, the Progressive movements and the New Deal had brought libertarianism into eclipse, though it never lacked for spirited champions like H. L. Mencken and A. J. Nock, nor economic defenders like Frank Knight of the Chicago School.

Certainly, though, the libertarian revolt of the 1940s caught most by sur-prise. It had its roots in Europe and in the emigré recoil from the horrors of totalitarianism. What would be known as the Austrian School of economists, Ludwig von Mises and Friedrich A. Hayek most influentially, articulated the case for the free market and against the dangers that lie in expanded state power. Hayek's book of 1944, *The Road to Serfdom*, argued powerfully that "planning leads to dictatorship" and he traced the European fascist move-ments back to their socialist beginnings. Hailed as "one of the great liberal sentiments of our time," Hayek's book caught on quickly in the United States. He in turn left his outpost in London and toured the United States broadcast-ing its message.[29] Other libertarian manifestos would follow—Mises' *Human Action* (1949) and Hayek's magisterial work, *The Constitution of Liberty* (1960).

In the 1960s and early 1970s, libertarianism found outspoken defenders in Ayn Rand, science fiction novelist Robert Heinlein, and Murray Rothbard. Rothbard made the most consistent ideological case for libertarianism, even denouncing conservatives for the anticommunist fears that had turned them toward the prosecutorial powers of the state. Rothbard's libertarianism was so unyielding that it drew the critical response of William F. Buckley, Jr.[30] Nonetheless, when Rothbard happened to have a conversation with a young Harvard professor, Robert Nozick, the professor decided to write a book.

Nozick took a circuitous route to libertarianism. In high school in the 1950s he had joined the youth branch of Norman Thomas's Socialist Party, and as an undergraduate at Columbia he founded another Socialist group. But Noz-ick gradually yielded to the persuasive forces of individualism and of moral and economic systems that gave highest priority to the free individual. He became persuaded that the case for that position had been made—by the Austrian economists and others. But none, he believed, had made the moral case for capitalism, at least not recently and not well. Hence *Anarchy, State, and Utopia.*[31]

Nozick's book is not an easy matter. It flourishes with the philosopher's love of dense logic-chopping and finely-tuned disputation. The reader will find many pages full of mathematical symbols. In its analytical depth it resembles the work of Nozick's rival Rawls. Nozick won respect for that effort. One reviewer called *Anarchy* "a major event in political philosophy." The reviewer noted that recent political theory generally assumed the necessary distributive role of the state. However correct, he added, after *Anarchy, State, and Utopia* these axioms could no longer be taken for granted.[32]

Rawls had asked the question, on what grounds *would* a people set up a state? Nozick wanted to ask the question, on what grounds *may* a people set up a state? His query led him to posit something like Rawls' original position, but Nozick's natural state had a more Hobbesian character. For the beginning human condition, he said, is one in which fear leads people to seek protection, essentially protection for their liberties, or against infringement of them by others. Out of this fear, one may assume that protective agencies emerge, to which one pays money or exchanges goods or services in return for protection provided by these groups. And out of this condition of competing protective agencies, one alone will almost certainly emerge as dominant. All of this unplanned activity, Nozick believed, had a legitimate and justifiable function. He also insisted that in this evolution one may locate the origins of a minimal state. This state differs from its predecessors only to the extent that it now claims to have a monopoly of the protective function. Nozick replied to the anarchist that a state may be justified on these grounds. But the burden of the rest of his book lay in Nozick's elaborate effort to show that the state may have justification *only* on these grounds. That is, it may emerge from protective associations on moral grounds, but it may acquire no other legitimation.[33]

Nozick summarized his argument to this point by certifying that no new individual rights emerge at the group level that did not exist at the prestate level, and that these rights center on personal liberty. That liberty included anyone's exemption from any forced obligation to participate in sharing activities determined by others. No one organization, e.g. the state, can act so as to give people benefits and then demand or seize payment from the rest for those purposes.

Nozick labeled the underlying principle of his book the "entitlement theory." (The term may be confusing, because in the 1980s "entitlements" referred to federal programs—such as Social Security or Medicaid—locked into the budget and referenced in discussions of the federal deficit and the problem of reducing it; Nozick, it will be clear, meant something quite different.) As he prepared to make the case against the distributive function of the state, Nozick wanted to establish securely on what grounds individuals could claim to hold what they had gained, what they could protect, on moral and legal grounds, from any state appropriation. His elaboration led eventually to this formulation:

1. A person who acquires a holding in accordance with the principle of justice in acquisition is entitled to the holding.
2. A person who acquires a holding in accordance with the principle of justice in transfer, from someone else entitled to that holding, is entitled to the holding.
3. No one is entitled to a holding except by (repeated) applications of 1 and 2.[34]

Furthermore, Nozick used this principle to distinguish his idea of justice from others'. The entitlement principle, he said, is historical; it asks how things came into being. Rival, distributive principles ask how things ought to be. They apply structural considerations. Nozick called these principles "end-result" or "end-state" principles. To illustrate, Nozick referred to current welfare programs as reflecting end-state applications. They are redistributive according to an abstract or arbitrary scheme of exchange payments. In contrast, Nozick, borrowing from Hayek, pointed to the ad hoc system of exchange, including bequests and contributions to charity, and called it effective and reasonable. "The system of entitlements," he wrote, "is defensible when constituted by the individual aims of individual transactions. No overarching aim is needed, no distributional pattern is required."[35] Nozick wanted to impress that any end-state theory of justice is unattainable short of continuous interference in people's lives.[36]

Nozick gave some fifty pages of his book to a critique of John Rawls. He had, to be sure, much respect for his Harvard colleague, and he called *A Theory of Justice* "a powerful, deep, subtle, wide-ranging, systematic work in political and moral philosophy."[37] But he also attacked the very premises of Rawls' treatise. Recall that Rawls, in perhaps the most appealing attribute of his theory, placed a priority on the least advantaged of society, and made it the focus of his difference principle. (First Nozick queried Rawls as to why he focused on groups and not on the least advantaged *individual*.)[38] Nozick took Rawls to be giving the least advantaged a kind of veto power over the better off and their activities. ("We will permit your gains, only if we also gain.") But as a logical and moral proposition, Nozick could not see why the better off could not also make such a demand, why they could not say, we'll cooperate with you so long as *we* are better off. Here Nozick became untypically blunt. "Why shouldn't the better endowed," he asked, "treat [Rawls' conditions] as beneath consideration, supposing someone to have the nerve explicitly to state it?" Of course, Nozick considered either claim invalid.[39]

Rawls hoped that his theory would show how different groups might enter into a society and stay in it on mutually agreeable terms. But Nozick believed that Rawlsian ideals led to only greater antagonisms. They did so in the more obvious tensions created between the least advantaged and the better off, but also in a manner that created endless conflict. Nozick's dealing with this matter typifies the acute logic that prevails in *Anarchy*. The group (in Rawls's society) that is next above the least advantaged group, Nozick said, will want to eliminate that group, so that it (the higher group) will be the measure of the fairness principle. So Nozick wrote, in a footnote observation: "The difference principle [i.e. Rawls'] thus creates *two* conflicts of interest: between those at the top and those at the bottom; *and* between those in the middle and those at the bottom, for if those at bottom were gone the difference principle might apply to improve the position of those in the middle, who would become the new bottom group whose position is to be maximized."[40]

Nozick believed he saw in Rawls at least two troubling biases that underscored his theory. Rawls, he said, looked at the inequality in society and assumed that it derived from natural assets in people, assets "arbitrary from a moral perspective."[41] But Rawls in this way ignored the question of what people had done with the natural assets they have received. "Why is that simply left out?" he asked. The biological and social determinism Nozick perceived in Rawls troubled him considerably. He found it also inconsistent with a theory that purported to buttress the dignity and self-respect of individuals, for it offered instead only a shallow and demeaning view of human power, choice, and responsibility.[42]

Also, Nozick could not understand why Rawls, or myriad like-minded liberals, focused so much on equality. Why was it necessary so painstakingly to justify any inequality or difference in persons? Inequality, Nozick said, must invariably enter into everything we do. If I go to one movie theater and not to the one next door to it, have I not treated the unpatronized theater unequally? Such free activity needs no justification, Nozick argued, but a government, compelling behavior of all, somehow does. Nozick's entitlement theory of justice, on the other hand, made no presumption in favor of equality. It supplied Nozick a major point of contrast to current end-state theories. Ultimately, he believed, Rawls' own end-state theory was morally deficient.[43]

Finally, among the many other considerations, Nozick addressed the question of economic and political power. He did so in a section in which he answered traditional arguments for extending state power beyond the minimal conditions that Nozick laid out early in the book. Contemporary liberalism seemed to assume that economic power translated into political power, Nozick noted, and hence justified the watch guard state. It must certify that money does not purchase extra political privilege. For Nozick, that argument turned the minimal state into the maximum state. He wrote: "the illegitimate use of a state by economic interests for their own ends is based upon a preexisting illegitimate power of the state to enrich some persons at the expense of others." Nozick even credited radical historians for showing the inherently unneutral character of government, its capacity to be the tool of the rich and powerful. The main point, at least, was clear: "Eliminate *that* illegitimate power of giving differential economic benefits and you eliminate or drastically restrict the motive for wanting political interest." The minimal state thus reduces the chances for the corrupting liaison of economic power and political influence.[44]

Anarchy, State, and Utopia offered a theoretical, philosophical defense of libertarianism. It could chop an argument a thousand ways to that end. It often gave illustrations, but too often came up short of details. Nonetheless, reviewers took Nozick's book to be, ultimately, a polemic against all the apparatus of the *modern* liberal state—welfare operations, public health care, compulsory social security, state-sponsored education, progressive taxation, and legislated equality of any kind.[45] Some conservatives therefore welcomed Nozick's ideas. But Nozick wanted to be consistent. His libertarianism, however welcomed by conservative businessmen, for example, aspired to give them no privileges. Nozick insisted that he opposed any government favoritism, as, for example, in subsidies to businesses (the airlines) or in protective tariffs. He opposed antidrug laws, but also wondered why radical youth who demanded free sex did not also celebrate free enterprise.[46] True and consistent libertarianism, like Nozick's, always confounds the liberal-conservative dichotomies.

Afterword

The term *postmodern* assumed a descriptive role in several categories of American thought and culture in the 1970s. Often influenced greatly by European formulations, it always acquired an American vernacular as native practitioners and theorists gave it their own descriptions. In the late 1970s and 1980s, postmodernism acquired a systematizing role in intellectual discourse. It came to express a more fundamental condition of contemporary life and culture. It could carry heavy ideological content, to be sure, for postmodernism as a normative reference to life in the late twentieth century invited both analysis and polemics. From Europe many intellectuals—Jean-Francois Lyotard, Jürgen Habermas, Jean Baudrillard, Christopher Norris, and others—continued to have an American impact. But two American thinkers, in turn, made major contributions to the postmodernist turn in the West.

Fredric Jameson, as seen earlier, contributed significantly to discussions of literary theory in the 1970s, and in the next decade took on the postmodern as a social and cultural subject, beginning with a 1983 essay, "Postmodernism and Consumer Society."[1] Jameson expanded his ideas for his 1991 book *Postmodernism: or, the Cultural Logic of Late Capitalism*, an ambitious undertaking that discussed economics, art and architecture, cinema, literature, and related matters. The book won a special award from the Modern Language Association.

Jameson's work represents the most important effort to interpret postmodernism in a Marxist framework. That intellectual tradition, we have observed, met a severe challenge from postmodernist thinkers in the 1970s. Writing in the 1980s, Jameson felt the challenge even more acutely. One example of the challenge was Lyotard, "*the* postmodernist *par excellence*."[2] Lyotard had a career in French politics, from trade union activity to Algerian liberationist advocacy, and he worked with the group "Socialisme ou Barbarie." By the late

1970s he had defined a radical postmodernism. He inveighed against all totalities and brought his critical stance into discussions of language systems and discourse. He judged metanarrative of any kind the linguistic symbol and corollary of all systems of power. He described rationalism as an intellectual vehicle of capitalist cultural and economic control—capital as reason incarnate. Lyotard included Marxism as a category in liberal rationalism. In tune with the postmodernist French Left generally, he described Marxism as part and parcel of the grand narrative power of Western political programming. He granted Marxism some critical distance, but asserted that in practice its character as a metanarrative of history led to the horrors that attended its implementation. Marxism supplied for Lyotard a totalizing model of knowledge with totalizing effects. To the postmodernist Left, Marxism signified suppression of difference.[3]

Jameson confronted the postmodernist challenge to Marxism by placing postmodernism itself under severe scrutiny. He rejected the equation of postmodernism with difference, variety, tolerance, and freedom. Instead, he correlated postmodernism with the immense controlling power of late capitalism. To understand postmodernism, he believed, one must correlate the new cultural expressions with the new forms of economic production and organization. Jameson would restore the base/superstructure to critical analysis and show how postmodern culture itself reflects economics. And as a Marxist, Jameson feared that unless one relocated a cultural dominant in the postmodern situation, one would have only the sense of heterogeneity, random difference, and accident as a prevailing norm, a norm ipso facto defiant of any reformist response.[4]

Postmodernism signified certain key cultural changes to Jameson. Looking at postmodernist architecture—figures such as Robert Venturi and John Portman—and at painting—movements such as pop art and photo realism—Jameson noted first a clear shift from modernism. He located that shift in the effacement of the older demarcations between high culture and so-called mass culture, or commercial culture. Postmodernism had a distinct tone and feel about it. "The postmodernists have, in fact," Jameson wrote, "been fascinated precisely by [the] whole 'degraded' landscape of schlock and kitsch." Jameson meant by this reference television and *Reader's Digest* culture, advertising, the grade-B Hollywood film, pulp novels.[5]

Associated with this condition, Jameson found that postmodernism conveyed a certain flatness, depthlessness. These qualities differentiated it from high modernism. Postmodernism did not convey differentiations of space and time, it did not invoke classic modernist norms such as anxiety or alienation, and it dissolved the radical subjectivity, even the madness, of the modernist subject. Modernism, too, as in literature, projected complexity and ambiguity of language, irony. It constructed elaborate symbolic systems. In contrast, Jameson wrote, postmodernism lacks "interpretive depth." "All these effects," Jameson believed, evoked the fashionable, contemporary theme of the "death of the subject," and Jameson readily associated that phenomenon with the passing of the bourgeois individual, the self-defined ego of the emergent capitalist society. "Late" capitalism, denoted by its massive international structures and organizational bureaucracy, has these qualities of the postmodern; it reflects, he said, "the whole new decentered global network of the third stage of capital itself." Jameson described this correlative:

> The end of the bourgeois ego, or monad, no doubt brings with it the end of the psychopathologies of that ego . . . the end, for example, of style, in the sense of the unique and the personal, the end of the distinctive individual brushstroke. . . . As for expression and feelings and emotions, the liberation, in contemporary society, from the older anomie of the centered subject may also mean not only a liberation from anxiety but a liberation from every other kind of feeling as well, since there is no longer a self present to do the feeling.[6]

These features, too, distinguished postmodernism from modernism. Jameson could describe modernist literature or painting as the privileged forms of capitalist culture. Bourgeois subjectivity reigned in these expressions. But they also conveyed capitalism's political unconscious. They disclose a process of disintegration in which the bourgeois subject makes its last stand of resistance against the consuming commodification of all cultural expression. Modernism, then, yields naturally and inevitably to postmodernism. Jameson doubted that high modernist art, which had preserved its power by distancing itself from consumer society, could even now exist. Postmodernism, the cultural reflection of late capitalism, obliterates all boundaries between high and low art. No critical distance remains. We live amid the total aestheticization of everyday life.[7]

The demise of the personal style, Jameson believed, also prompts the postmodernist recourse to pastiche, the ransacking of history for reappropriation of atavistic forms, mostly in a stereotypical rendering. There results, said Jameson, the random play of stylistic allusion, and with it the flattening out of time. We have only a haphazard eclecticism, free-floating signifiers abstracted from an historical flea market. Jameson saw that pattern exemplified in the nostalgia films of the 1970s. Altogether, though, this phenomenon, Jameson believed, demonstrated a waning of historicity. The experience of history under postmodern conditions loses its depth and feel, becomes ephemerality. The historical artifact becomes the merely decorative, providing only a spurious sense of rootedness, an escape from anxiety and alienation.[8]

The French writer Jean Baudrillard also described postmodernist reality in terms of a total domination of signs. Baudrillard's writings, from the late sixties on, had given him, by the end of the eighties, "guru status throughout the English-speaking world," as his works became translated. It was said of Baudrillard that he "has developed the most striking and extreme theory of postmodernity yet produced."[9] In his writings of the early 1970s, Baudrillard discussed such subjects as cybernetics, media, information technologies, and art and architecture. With his *For a Critique of the Political Economy of the State* in 1972, Baudrillard fell into unavoidable tensions with Marxism. The new culture of the sign, he believed, disqualified almost all previous models of social analysis, Marxist among them. Baudrillard claimed that the traditional Marxist dichotomies—subject-object, base-superstructure, exploitation-alienation— had been so thoroughly dissolved as to have become meaningless. The whole dominant pattern of the commodity culture, Baudrillard believed, had to be rendered as a sign system before any understanding of its social operations and effects could make any sense at all. Baudrillard wrote:

> It is because the structure of the sign is at the very heart of the commodity format the commodity can take on, immediately, the effect of signification: not epiphenominally, in excess of itself, as "message" or connotation, but because its very form establishes it as a total *medium*, as a *system of communication* administering all social exchange. Like the sign form, the commodity is a code managing the exchange of values. . . . [I]t is the code that is determinant: the rules of the interplay of signifiers and exchange value.[10]

Baudrillard, in short, described in postmodernism a new historical departure and a new paradigm of social analysis. In modernity, he said, we experienced an era of production controlled by the industrial bourgeoisie. The postmodern era establishes a system of information and signs governed by models, codes, and cybernetics in which signs take on a life of their own. They erode the once assumed differentiation of the real and the image, the object and its facsimile. They call into question all prevailing notions of representation. In the postmodern world, Baudrillard explained, the very existence of the "real" dissolves. This, the last stage of capitalism, introduces the prevailing culture of "hyperreality," the culture in which simulations constitute reality itself.[11]

Jameson, too, saw a postmodernist reign of simulacra. He characterized the dominant images as flat, one-dimensional, temporally thin and thus altogether resistant to interpretation. He concurred with Baudrillard that they resisted all interpretive engagement and all cultural criticism. For Jameson, postmodernity reflected a condition in which, as in structuralism and poststructuralism, the sign has been detached from its referent. It has no connection to it or dependence upon it. In the age of media, advertising, television, videos all has become a free play of signs, a *jouissance* of anarchic pseudoreality. Postmodernism posits the radical separation of the signifier from the signified.[12]

For Jameson this postmodern "reality" clearly referenced an underlying totality comprehensible from a Marxist perspective and demanding Marxist judgment. Jameson thus urged that what appears to be the demise of the cultural, its status of relative autonomy, should be seen in fact as its extension into the entire social realm. The "cultural" has no precise, defining boundaries, as Baudrillard had noted, and everything from economics to politics falls under the rubric. In the age of television and the advertising media, everything is cultural, the culture of the commodity. Jameson believed it was in this sense, precisely, that capitalism secures its greatest hegemony. For the effects of this undifferentiating are the loss of any distancing, any critical removal, within the postmodernist art product from commercialized life. Globally, Jameson observed, every aspect of the precapitalist era has, under the conditions of late, or international capitalism, succumbed to these colonizing effects. Nature and the unconscious are not exempt. Nothing remains of uncommodified space. "What we must now affirm," wrote Jameson, "is that it is precisely this whole extraordinary demoralizing and depressing original new global space which is the 'moment of truth' of postmodernism."[13]

By historicizing the postmodern, Jameson reclaimed for Marxism its critical effectiveness, and this especially against its postmodernist critics on the Left. For by this route, Jameson restored the reality of the totality against all its postmodernist incursions, preserving Marxism's major dogmatic feature. For the leftist position, that effort would seem to have considerable significance. As a writer sympathetic to Jameson has pointed out, a radical postmodernism may err in overvalorizing plurality, fragmentation, and pluralism. "The unqualified rejection of holism, systemic analysis, and totality as a normative concept," this writer said, "reproduces the alienation and fragmentation capitalism has already brought to social life." Without some counterbalance, he added, "we are abandoned to the seriality of pluralist individualism and the supremacy of competitive values over communal life."[14] Jameson used a reconstructed Marxism to expose the postmodernist program.

Richard Rorty, professor of philosophy at Princeton and then at the University of Virginia, wrote two books that established his significance for the 1970s. Fortified in the 1980s by many more contributions, his repertoire made him one of the most discussed philosophers of that decade. His collection of essays, *Consequences of Pragmatism* (all but two of the twelve written in the 1970s), and his major treatise, *Philosophy and the Mirror of Nature* (1979), reinforced each other in Rorty's sustained effort to rethink the enterprise of philosophy and to suggest its larger uses for modern life. Rorty's significance in the 1980s is indicated by the large volume of responses made to his ideas in the anthology edited by Alan Malachowski, *Reading Rorty*, published in England in 1990.[15] Rorty's system revised the American philosophical tradition and made important overtures to American political liberalism. He thus continues the discussion of the previous chapter.

It matters critically, Rorty said, just how one sees the history of philosophy. For the most part, Westerners, he believed, had got it all wrong. Philosophy under Western eyes had long sought to make itself the foundational system of all thinking and even the underlying, validating source of all other disciplines. For a long time that effort meant that philosophy would endeavor to represent accurately what is outside the mind, the essential nature of reality. In the Enlightenment, that quest assumed a special significance for now philosophy succeeded religion as the surer foundation of ultimate truth, a surrogate role that it gladly took on for itself.[16]

Although most historians of philosophy attribute to Kant a paradigm shift, Rorty, while recognizing his great significance, sees an essential continuity. Kant relocated philosophy from its concern with an exterior reality to a focus on epistemology, a science of the mind and a grounding of its conditions and limitations. Thus, what began with Descartes and Spinoza now became a self-conscious pursuit in philosophy. But the neo-Kantian consensus, Rorty argued, really marks the end-product of the effort to make philosophy the Mirror of Nature. It inherits from Kant's predecessors a sense of knowledge as an assemblage of accurate representations, mind as the Mirror of Nature. But Kant creates the successor need to find, within the Mirror, a special class of representations whose authority cannot be doubted. He thus set philosophy to inspecting, polishing, and repairing the Mirror, as it were. Rorty: "These privileged foundations will be the foundation of knowledge, and the discipline which directs us toward them—the theory of knowledge—will be the foundations of culture. The theory of knowledge will be the search for that which compels the mind to belief as soon as it is unveiled. Philosophy-as-epistemology will be the search for immutable structures within which knowledge, life, and culture must be contained—structures set by the privileged representations which it studies." Now the path to contemporary structuralism lay clear ahead.[17]

As the Kantian tradition waned at the end of the century some philosophers turned to mathematical logic to rescue their subject from its various infections. Bertrand Russell and Edmund Husserl alternatively offered "logical form" and "essences," and philosophy, through these new privileged representations, renewed its quest for seriousness, purity, and rigor. By this time, Rorty could see much of modern philosophy as a continuum from Descartes, however various its expressions. These endeavors isolated inquiry prior to the empirical conclusions of inquiry. In this habit Rorty saw Western philosophy's most troubling character, its essentially ahistorical nature. Philosophy became a species of apologetics; it froze reality through privileged forms, logical structures, or linguistic devices. Even positivists fell into the postulating of essences, seeking to secure their systems on some formulaic depiction of human nature and to reduce knowable reality to some basically simple, descriptive content. All these efforts Rorty described by calling them Philosophy—capital *P*.[18]

Nonetheless, Rorty saw in the Western tradition a rival current and he hoped to reestablish its influence. Hegel had particular significance for Rorty in historicizing all philosophical efforts, asserting the relativity of ideas and language to a place and time, and anticipating the modern axiom that every-thing can be changed by talking in new terms.[19] Rorty also looked to Heidegger and to the later Ludwig Wittgenstein for philosophers testifying against Philosophy. Heidegger especially explored the way in which the West became obsessed with mind/object relations as analogous to visual perception.[20]

Rorty's link to Heidegger would prove crucial. It would enable him to recon-nect to American liberalism by means of Continental philosophy, especially through Heidegger, Derrida, and the poststructuralists. Rorty's essay "Over-coming the Tradition: Heidegger and Dewey" made a beginning effort. He saw both philosophers attempting to set aside the main foundations of Western thought and offer something new. Both became "historicist to the core" in doing so. Both penetrated through the obscuring essences that Western thought had privileged everywhere and they had tried to recover what Heidegger called "beings-without-Being" or what Dewey called the problematical aspects of our ordinary experience. So when joined with Wittgenstein, Dewey and Heidegger make a formidable assault on the logocentric character of Western thinking, the representational effort embodied in the Mirror analogy. These three thinkers, wrote Rorty, emphasize "the holistic point that words take their meaning from other words rather than by virtue of their representative character."[21] Here for Rorty was the critical undertaking: "We must get the visual, and in particular the mirroring, metaphors out of our speech altogether."[22]

Rorty's efforts took him to language theory and to Heidegger, Hans-Georg Gadamer, Foucault, and Derrida particularly. He quoted from them and solicited their help in detaching philosophy from its mirror habits. "The authors cited," wrote Rorty " . . . are saying that attempts to get back behind language to something which 'grounds' it, or which it 'expresses,' or to which it might hope to be 'adequate,' have not worked." Gadamer and Derrida, in discrediting the notion of a "transcendental signifier," and Foucault, in joining Nietzsche in moving out from under the "metaphysical comfort" provided by traditional Philosophy, all assisted Rorty in his wish to derail philosophy from its preoccupation with ultimate truth.[23]

Rorty sided with those who wanted to liberate the text from narrow codes and confined readings. He cited Foucault and Harold Bloom as "strong mis-readers" who encouraged getting more out of a text than an author could have given or an intended audience could have found in it. Wrote Rorty: "The strong misreader doesn't care about the distinction between discovery and creation, finding and making. He doesn't think this is a useful distinction, any more than Nietzsche or James did. He is in it for what he can get out of it, not for the satisfaction of getting something right."[24] If that sounded like Niet-zsche or William James, all the better. It took Rorty another step back toward American pragmatism. The movement that Rorty called "textualism" is most usefully understood, Rorty believed, "as an attempt to think through a thor-ough-going pragmatism, a thorough-going abandonment of the notion of *dis-covering the truth* which is common to theology and science."[25]

When Rorty asked of his vocation that it enter a post-Philosophical era he outlined more completely what he wanted philosophy to do and he described the characteristics he wanted it to acquire. Philosophy, he urged, must move beyond its epistemological efforts and become a hermeneutical activity. Then it abandons the quest for the conditioning groundwork of all thinking or for some antecedently existing common ground of agreement, a universal basis for knowing. Hermeneutics takes a more relaxed and playful approach. It accepts all the contingencies that make for variety, all the chance factors that have somehow acted to create a community, and it asks how they hold together. It will see all language and discourse as a kind of conversation, rather than as a structure, one into which philosophy itself enters. Properly conducted, philosophy as hermeneutics destabilizes all foundational conditions and properties only to rebuild knowledge along historicist lines. This kind of understanding is akin to getting acquainted with someone, Rorty explained. It seeks familiarity by taking a peripheral look at things; it aspires to make us more at home in our world. "Hermeneutics," wrote Rorty, " . . . is what we get when we are no longer epistemological."[26]

Hermeneutics is also what we get when philosophy abandons Philosophy, that is, when the Mirror of Nature no longer provides the discipline's dominant analogy. The Mirror had defined for Philosophy its ways of knowing. Rorty now argued that philosophy does not signify a way of knowing; it signifies a way of coping. And that emphasis, too, led Rorty to pragmatism, the descriptions of philosophy given by Americans Charles Sanders Peirce, William James, and especially John Dewey. Pragmatism had used the language of Darwinism to derive its key notions of the survival value of ideas, of mind as a tool of adaptation, of thought as a means of adaptation and adjustment, or of simply getting us where we want to go. The pragmatist, Rorty wrote, drops the notion of truth as correspondence with reality. He says that modern science does not enable us to cope because it corresponds; "it just plain enables us to cope." Philosophy becomes a way of seeing how the world lies, how it hangs together, and how we make our way through it.[27]

"Pragmatists are saying that the best hope for philosophy is not to practice Philosophy," wrote Rorty. When it no longer does so, he argued, philosophy will enter its post-Philosophy situation. That situation will create a certain discomfort because in it men and women will feel alone, with no connections to any Truth, no ties to something Beyond. But in forsaking that kind of comfort, philosophy will seek another kind of security, the more mundane and less dramatic one of simply knowing where we are in the world. In a post-Philosophical culture what we call knowledge will provide us with only "temporary resting-places." And knowledge, too, will be more than Philosophy or science. In the post-Philosophical situation, the poet and the storyteller and the artist will be our seers; they will all show us the world as found.[28]

Rorty knew how some would consider this role of philosophy and this view of knowledge. The Platonists, he said, will see such a culture as having no ruling principle, no center or structure. The positivists will see it as having no respect for hard fact, as too "cultural" and insufficiently "scientific." Both dissenters would see this pragmatism as lacking guidance, either by some eternal principle or notion of good or truth, or by reason and scientific criteria. Some might see in it a kind of decadence. Rorty had to impress on his readers that post-Philosophy is no less "noble" a work than its predecessors'.[29]

In Continental thinkers such as Heidegger, Foucault, and Derrida, Rorty saw the path that philosophy should follow. They saw the arts and literature as the key insights into any historical condition. And with the radical skepticism that each of these thinkers brought to the Western intellectual tradition, Rorty could reference their work for his own purposes. And yet, for all their significance, Rorty used the Continental thinkers ultimately to return to the American Dewey. Postmodernism revisits pragmatism. Dewey, Rorty believed, anticipated almost everything important in Heidegger, Foucault, and Derrida. But Dewey could claim a higher merit in being more historicist than any of them, in making experience more central to his thought. Rorty's pragmatism makes the opening to the new thought only to domesticate it, to "Americanize" it. Post-Philosophy will turn out after all to have a very familiar ring to it.[30]

It acquired that familiarity above all when Rorty made it the basis of a revived liberalism, to which he gave more attention in the early 1980s. Thus, for example, Rorty believed that if we understood what postmodernist thought meant by the "self," a term important to historic liberalism, we may appropriate certain advantages from it. Rorty wanted to add to liberalism the notion of the "decentered self," as opposed to an older idea of the essential self. The latter connoted a kind of transcendent "real" self that it became the object of each of us to realize, a sort of noumenal entity waiting to be attained when all the unessential aspects of our phenomenal self were overcome. But that idea simply echoed all the philosophical habits that Rorty wished to abandon. His idea of the self paralleled the description given by American deconstructionist Jonathan Culler. "As it is deconstructed, broken down into systems that are all trans-subjective, the self or subject comes to appear more as a construct: the result of systems of convention. When man speaks, he artfully 'complies with language'; language speaks through him. . . . The 'I' is not something given; it comes to exist."[31]

Rorty, however, refused to see the linguistic foundation as anything deterministic. Rorty offered an aestheticized self as opposed to an essential self, and intended by it a self created. This self is made out of the materials of the entire cultural field available to the individual. Creativity, in turn, requires new ways of saying things, new modes of descriptions. Rorty looked to Nietzsche and his demand that we create new worlds though new vocabularies, that we "create ourselves as a work of art." Derrida, Rorty believed, meant the same thing in saying that we should learn "to inhabit old structures in new ways." The "aesthetic ideal" for Rorty meant "self-enlargement" as opposed to "self-purification."[32]

This kind of creativity, self-creativity, involved for Rorty a measure of play. Here his liberalism assumed emblematic postmodernist effects. Once we remove from philosophy its earnest pursuit of ultimate truth or ultimate moral law we can approach the world playfully. Rorty called for "light-minded aestheticism." He welcomed the "insouciant pluralism" of contemporary culture. Especially in language was this insouciance needful. Rorty appreciated Derrida's efforts to liberate language from the transcendental signifier outside the text, whose essence lies outside the language. Derrida approached language and used language with *jouissance*, employing multilingual puns, humor, free-floating allusions, and phonic and typographical gimmicks. "Derrida does not want to comprehend Hegel's books," Rorty wrote; "he wants to play with Hegel."[33]

In passing through the poststructuralists back to Dewey, Rorty wished to save key ingredients of American liberalism. In comparing Dewey and Foucault, for example, Rorty observed that both made the same criticisms of the philosophical tradition. They agreed on the need to abandon traditional notions of rationality, objectivity, method, and truth and concurred that these things are what history and society make them—there is no overarching ahistorical structure as embodied in "The Nature of Man," the "Moral Law," and the like, waiting to be discovered. But Foucault represents for Rorty the "dark side" of this understanding. He sees language as a determinant of power and reads it back into patterns of domination. With Foucault, all knowledge claims exist, as they did for Nietzsche, as moves in a power-game. Dewey, by contrast, saw the move "beyond method" as liberating; it gives humankind an opportunity to advance, a freedom to make itself, a new responsibility for mastery, free now from preoccupation with some imagined outside source of sustenance and dependency. "In Dewey's hands," Rorty wrote, "the will to truth is not the urge to dominate but the urge to create."[34]

By taking philosophy to a primary concern for aesthetic self-creation, Rorty highlighted in his postmodernist liberalism a strong libertarian and individualistic quality. His liberalism had much less of the collectivist quality than that of John Rawls, although more of the communitarian ideal than that of Robert Nozick. Rorty's community consisted of selves in a common need to get along, to work things out. It got along by seeing things fresh and new and deriving a discourse by which to adjust to them. But there is not much more than that to hold it together, and there need not be, Rorty believed. He supported "a public ethic of accommodation" against "a private ethic of self-creation." But that ethic still left a real priority for the individual. And good for the individual, he said, comes through the unhindered freedom for self-enlargement by means of idiosyncratic self-descriptions. To the group he conceded only the need to protect its band of hearty eccentrics, each in pursuit of his and her own individual self-enlargement.[35]

The ideal culture, then, "has no ideal except freedom." For Rorty, liberty must exist and we must take it where we will, whatever the consequences.

Society must exist for the "poets and revolutionaries" in its midst, even though that same liberty may give us mostly bland and unheroic individuals. To that extent, Rorty believed, we should not suffer "all the nasty things about bourgeois liberalism" that its enemies have taught us. In his essay "Philosophy in America Today," Rorty wrote: "On my view, we should be more willing than we are to celebrate bourgeois capitalist society as the best polity actualized so far, while regretting that it is irrelevant to most of the problems of most of the population of the planet." Bourgeois liberalism, said Rorty, must preserve the conditions for self-creativity, and although he welcomed poets and revolutionaries, he acknowledged too that all inquiry must begin with "the way *we* live now," with the language and convictions central to our liberal democracy.[36] By the early 1980s Rorty was pleased to be the defender of "postmodernist bourgeois liberalism."[37] Americans might ponder what those words mean. As the United States keeps a rendezvous with the twenty-first century that ideal might best assure the American tradition a viable future.

Chronology

1970   "Chicago Seven" trial ends with sentencing of defendants. Americans celebrate first "Earth Day." Four antiwar students at Kent State University die from National Guard shooting. FBI labels Black Panthers America's most dangerous group. Alvin Toffler publishes *Future Shock*. Antiwar radicals bomb Army research building on University of Wisconsin campus. The Carpenters' "Close to You" is the number one single record in September. Chile elects Marxist Salvador Allende as president. Congress creates the Public Broadcasting System. Rock singer Janis Joplin dies of apparent heroin overdose. Alexander Solzhenitsyn awarded Nobel Prize for literature. Charles Reich publishes counterculture manifesto *The Greening of America*. Beatles singer George Harrison releases *All Things Must Pass* in December. *Monday Night Football* debuts. *Love Story* brings tears to American moviegoers. University of Wisconsin scientists perform the first complete synthesis of a gene. IBM introduces the floppy disk, a computer storage device. California passes the first no-fault divorce law.

1971   Hot pants become fashion rage for female Smart Set. *Patton* wins seven Oscars. Five thousand march in New York City Gay Rights parade. Supreme Court allows *New York Times* to publish *Pentagon Papers*. Riot at Attica prison in New York kills 28 prisoners. Intel of California introduces the microprocessor. The Illiac IV computer can handle 200 million instructions a second. The United States builds the world's largest proton accelerator in Batavia, Illinois. Cigarette advertising is banned from television. *Look* magazine ceases publication. The term "workaholic" enters the English language.

1972 Don McLean sings "American Pie." President Nixon makes historic visit to China in March. Senate supports proposed Equal Rights Amendment, 84-0. *The Last Whole Earth Catalogue* appears. Nixon orders heavy bombing of Hanoi and Haiphong, North Vietnam. In May, George Wallace is shot by Arthur Bremer. Roberta Flack sings "The First Time Ever I Saw Your Face." *Superfly* highlights vogue of black-centered movies. Swimmer Mark Spitz wins seven gold Olympic medals. Thomas Harris writes *I'm OK, You're OK*. Bobby Fischer wins world chess championship in September. Nixon carries 49 states in massive electoral victory over George McGovern. Stanley Kubrick presents movie *Clockwork Orange*. *Godfather* becomes blockbuster movie of the year. *Deep Throat* brings pornography to mass movie audience. Watergate scandal emerges. The undefeated Miami Dolphins win a record seventeen straight games.

1973 *All in the Family* redefines the television sit-com. Baseball's American League begins the designated hitter rule. Supreme Court issues controversial *Roe v. Wade* verdict supporting abortion. Roberta Flack sings "Killing Me Softly with His Song." *Ms*. magazine debuts. Senate begins Watergate hearings in June. Military coup deposes Allende in Chile. Arab nations inaugurate Yom Kippur war against Israel in October. American Psychiatric Association no longer considers homosexuality a mental disorder. Vice President Spiro Agnew resigns in October, Nixon names Gerald Ford to replace him. Nixon signs bill to build Alaskan oil pipeline. Oil-producing nations' embargo shocks American economy with doubling of oil prices. The movie *The Exorcist* induces hysteria among many of its viewers. *Pioneer X* approaches Jupiter and its relayed photographs detail the planet's red spot.

1974 "Streaking" becomes the newest campus rage. Newspaper heiress Patty Hearst is kidnapped by radical Symbionese Liberation Army. Stevie Wonder dominates Grammy awards. Henry Aaron of Atlanta Braves breaks Babe Ruth's home run record. Little League allows girls to play. Supreme Court rules that President Nixon must surrender White House tapes. Nixon resigns presidency on 8 August; Ford takes office. Ford calls inflation Public Enemy #1. Oakland A's win third straight World Series. CB (Citizens' Band) radio becomes a rage. Nelson Rockefeller becomes vice president. Ultrasound diagnostic techniques are developed. Episcopal bishops defy church law and ordain eleven women as priests.

1975 Cambodian capital falls to genocidal Khmer Rouge. Ford orders total evacuation of Vietnam; last Americans leave Saigon in May. *Jaws* becomes largest box office movie to date. Cable TV station HBO begins nation-wide programming. *Ragtime* tops best-seller list in

October. Leisure suits reach height of popularity, documenting the decade's "casual" look. The proverbial "typical" American family of father, housewife, and two children represents only seven percent of the population.

1976   *One Flew Over the Cuckoo's Nest* garners Oscars. Saul Bellow wins Nobel Prize for literature. U.S. celebrates bicentennial 4 July. The Bellamy Brothers sing "Let Your Love Flow." Romania's gymnast Nadia Comaneci dazzles Olympics audiences. Mao Zedong dies in September. Jimmy Carter is elected president. Movie *Rocky* celebrates blue-collar hero. The three-piece suit returns to fashion. *Charlie's Angels* makes television debut. Barbara Jordan is first black woman to keynote Democratic convention. Dr. Wayne Dyer writes pop-psychology hit *Your Erroneous Zones*. *Viking I* lands on Mars and returns colorful photographs of landscape. The Apple computer emerges from a California garage.

1977   *Roots* becomes best-seller success. Carter holds first "town meeting" in March. Miami voters reject gay rights ordinance. Electricity failure in New York spurs looting and massive confusion. Carter says B-1 bomber is unnecessary. Chinese Communist party denounces Gang of Four, including wife of the late Mao. U.S. signs treaty that will relinquish control of Panama Canal. Elvis Presley dies at Graceland in August. Department of Energy is created. Former Columbia radical Mark Rudd surrenders after years underground. Movie *Star Wars* becomes largest revenue-earner to date. Carter pardons draft resisters.

1978   Carter defers neutron bomb. Hubert Humphrey dies at age 66 in January. Civil war spreads in Nicaragua. Rioting in Iran seeks ouster of the Shah. Atlantic City opens gambling casinos. Supreme Court delivers *Bakke* decision qualifying affirmative action programs in colleges. First "test tube" baby is born in England. House grants ERA deadline three-year extension. Fifty percent of all shoes sold are sneakers. Dollar loses badly to Japanese yen and German mark. Menachem Begin of Israel and Anwar Sadat of Egypt win Nobel Peace Prize. Religious cult commits mass suicide at People's Temple, Georgetown, Guyana. Movie *Deer Hunter* is released. Jim Fixx's *The Complete Book of Running* sells 620,000 copies. Medicine introduces balloon compression method of opening arteries. OPEC raises prices 14 percent. Inflation rate is 12.4 percent.

1979   Shah flees Iran and Ayatollah Khomeini establishes Islamic Republic. Jane Byrne becomes first woman mayor of Chicago. Three Mile Island nuclear accident. Margaret Thatcher becomes prime minister of Britain. First black government is elected in Rhodesia. Carter and Soviet leader Leonid Brezhnev sign Salt II treaty in June. Carter doubles Indochina refugee quota to 14,000 per month. Iranian students seize U.S. embassy in Tehran, take hostages. Carter decontrols domestic oil. Congress approves bailout for Chrysler. Soviet army invades Afghanistan in December. Gold reaches a record 524 dollars per ounce. Inflation is 13.3 percent.

Notes and References

Preface

1. See Susan Sontag, "Against Interpretation," in her collection of essays *Against Interpretation and Other Essays* (New York: Dell, 1967), 3-14; in the same volume, see also Sontag's "Notes on Camp," 275-92; and her "The Aesthetics of Silence," in *Styles of Radical Will* (London: Secker and Warburg, 1969), 3-34. For a useful intellectual history of postmodernism, see Hans Bertens, *The Idea of the Postmodern: A History* (London: Routledge, 1995).

2. See especially Leslie Fiedler, "The New Mutants," *Partisan Review* 32 (1965): 505-25; and Leslie Fiedler, "Cross the Border—Close that Gap—Postmodernism," in *American Literature Since 1900*, ed. Marcus Cunliffe (London: Sphere Books, 1975), 344-66; and Hans Bertens, *Idea of the Postmodern*, 29-31.

3. See Ihab Hassan, "Frontiers of Criticism: Metaphors of Silence," *Virginia Quarterly Review* 46 (1970):81-95; idem, *The Dismemberment of Orpheus: Toward a Postmodern Literature* (New York: Oxford University Press, 1971); idem, "The New Gnosticism: Speculations on an Aspect of the Postmodern Mind," *boundary* 3 (1971):547-69.

Chapter One

1. *The Third Century: America as a Post-Industrial Society*, ed. Seymour Martin Lipset (Stanford: Hoover Institution Press, 1979).

2. This and the following summary of postindustrialism are derived from the very useful account given by David Clark in his *Post-Industrial America: A Geographical Perspective* (New York: Methuen, 1985). The bibliography is particularly helpful.

3. See Paul Blumberg, *Inequality in an Age of Decline* (New York: Oxford University Press, 1980), pp. 155–59. For another pessimistic portrait of the postindustrial scene, see Harvey Braverman, *Labor and Monopoly Capital: The Degradation of Work in the Twentieth Century* (New York: Monthly Review Press, 1975).

4. Quoted in John Mack Faragher et al., *Out of Many: A History of the American People*, combined edition (Englewood Cliffs, N.J.: Prentice Hall, 1994), 966-67. I have borrowed material provided by this book for inclusion in this introduction.

5. Alvin Toffler, *Future Shock* (New York: Bantam Books, 1970), 37-38.

6. Ibid., 14-15.

7. Ibid., 17.

8. Ibid., 52-53.

9. Ibid., 64-65.

10. Ibid, 75-76, 80.

11. Daniel Bell, *The Coming of Post-Industrial Society: A Venture in Social Forecasting* (1973; reprint, New York: Basic Books, 1976), xii-xvii.

12. Ibid., 126.

13. Ibid., 126-27.

14. Ibid., 127-28.

15. Ibid., 18-20, 25, 44, 343-44.

16. Ibid., 344.

17. Ibid.

18. Ibid., 409-10.

19. Ibid., 426.

20. Ibid., 410, 416.

21. Ibid., 417.

22. Lasch contributed an earlier essay on postindustrialism. See Christopher Lasch, "Toward a Theory of Post-Industrial Society," in *Politics in the PostWelfare State: Responses to the New Individualism,* ed. M. Donald Hancock and Gideon Sjoberg (New York: Columbia University Press, 1972), 36-50.

23. Christopher Lasch, *The Culture of Narcissism: American Life in an Age of Diminishing Expectations* (New York: Warner Books, 1979), 18, 130-31, 21.

24. Ibid., 22-25.

25. Ibid., 33, 36.

26. Ibid., 46-47.

27. Ibid., 36-37, 64, 69.

28. Ibid., 96-97.

29. Ibid., 91-92.

30. Ibid., 150.

31. Ibid., 38-40.

Chapter Two

1. Ferdinand de Saussure, *Course in General Linguistics,* trans. Roy Harris (London: Duckworth, 1983), 110 as quoted in Art Berman, *From the New Criticism to Deconstruction: The Reception of Structuralism and Poststructuralism* (Urbana: University of Illinois Press, 1988), 115.

2. Quoted by Frank Lentricchia in *After the New Criticism* (Chicago: University of Chicago Press, 1980), 124.

3. Roland N. Stromberg, *After Everything: Western Intellectual History Since 1945* (New York: St. Martin's Press, 1975), 230; Terry Eagleton, *Literary Theory: An Introduction* (Minneapolis: University of Minnesota Press, 1983), 103-4; Lentricchia, *After the New Criticism,* 27; Ricoeur quoted by Lentricchia in *After the New Criticism,* 127.

4. Raman Selden, *A Reader's Guide to Contemporary Literary Theory* (Lexington: University Press of Kentucky, 1985), 52-53; Barthes quoted by Berman, *From the New Criticism,* 157.

5. Berman, *From the New Criticism,* 121.

6. Ibid., 118-21; Eagleton, *Literary Theory,* 10. 6-9.

7. Selden, *Contemporary Literary Theory,* 37-38; Berman, *From the New Criticism,* 157; Eagleton, *Literary Theory,* 109; Fredric Jameson, *The Prison-House of Language: A Critical Account of Structuralism and Russian Formalism* (Princeton: Princeton University Press, 1972).

8. Robert Scholes, *Structuralism in Literature: An Introduction* (New Haven: Yale University Press, 1974).

9. Jonathan Culler, *Structuralist Poetics: Structuralism, Linguistics, and the Study of Literature* (Ithaca: Cornell University Press, 1975); Christopher Norris, *Deconstruction: Theory and Practice* (London: Routledge, 1982), 2-3.

10. Hayden V. White, *Metahistory: The Historical Imagination in the Nineteenth Century* (Baltimore: Johns Hopkins University Press, 1973), ix-x.

11. Ibid., xii, 5-6, 31-38, 283-84.

12. Ibid., 1.

13. Selden, *Contemporary Literary Theory,* 72-73; Berman, *From the New Criticism,* 169; Eagleton, *Literary Theory,* 127-28.

14. Eagleton, *Literary Theory,* 129.

15. Berman, *From the New Criticism,* 133-34; Eagleton, *Literary Theory,* 129.

16. Berman, *From the New Criticism,* 208.

17. Saul Cornell, "Splitting the Difference: Textualism, Contextualism, and Post-Modern History," *American Studies* 36 (Spring 1995), 57-58.

18. Edward Said, *Beginnings: Intention and Method* (Baltimore: Johns Hopkins University Press, 1975), 284.

19. Ibid., 285.

20. Ibid., 287.

21. Ibid., 293.

22. Ibid., 297, 313.

23. Clifford Geertz, "Intellectual Roots," in *Assessing Cultural Anthropology,* ed. Robert Borofsky (New York: McGraw-Hill, 1973), 466.

24. Clifford Geertz, *The Interpretation of Cultures: Selected Essays* (New York: Basic Books, 1973), 38.

25. Ibid., 44-45.

26. Ibid., 47-51.

27. Ibid., 448-49.

28. Ibid., 449n.

29. George E. Marcus and Michael Fischer, *Anthropology as Cultural Critique: An Experimental Moment in the Human Sciences* (Chicago: University of Chicago Press, 1986), 35, 38.

30. Marvin Harris, "Cultural Materialism Is Alive and Well and Won't Go Away Until Something Better Comes Along," in *Assessing Cultural Anthropology,* 76-77.

31. Geertz, "The Uses of Diversity," in *Assessing Cultural Anthropology,* 457.

32. [J. Hillis Miller], "J. Hillis Miller on Literary Criticism," *New Republic,* 29 November 1975, 31-32.

33. On phenomenology, see Eagleton, *Literary Theory,* 54-90; Lentricchia, *After the New Criticism,* 62-101; on existentialism, see Lentricchia, *After the New Criticism,* 28-60 and Berman, *From the New Criticism,* 69-77.

34. Berman, *From the New Criticism,* 23; Poulet and Miller quoted by Cain, *Crisis in Criticism,* 33-34.

35. Miller quoted in Grant Webster, "J. Hillis Miller," in *Modern American Critics*, ed. Gregory S. Jay (Detroit: Gale Research Co., 1988), 226; see also, Donald Pease, "The Other Victorians at Yale," in Jonathan Arac et al., eds., *The Yale Critics: Deconstruction in America* (Minneapolis: University of Minnesota Press), 68.

36. Miller, quoted by Webster, "J. Hillis Miller," 226; see also Pease, "The Other Victorians," 68.

37. Berman, *From the New Criticism*, 233.

38. J. Hillis Miller, "Tradition and Difference," review of *Natural Supernaturalism: Tradition and Revolution in Romantic Literature*, by M. H. Abrams, *Diacritics* 2 (Winter 1972):6.

39. M. H. Abrams, *Natural Supernaturalism: Tradition and Revolution in Romantic Literature* (New York: Norton, 1971), 13, 46-51, 66.

40. Miller, "Tradition and Difference," 9.

41. Ibid., 11.

42. Ibid., 10.

43. Ibid.

44. Miller quoted by Berman, *From the New Criticism*, 231-32; Cain, *Crisis in Criticism*, 36; Robert Moynihan, [Interview with J. Hillis Miller], *Criticism* 24 (Spring 1982):114.

45. Moynihan, [Interview with J. Hillis Miller], 125.

46. Ibid., 130.

47. Pease, "The Other Victorians," 73-75.

48. Michael Sprinker, "Aesthetic Criticism," in *The Yale Critics*, 43-44.

49. Miller, "J. Hillis Miller on Literary Criticism," 34.

50. Geoffrey H. Hartman, "Monsieur Texte: Jacques Derrida: His Glas," *Georgia Review* 29 (1975):760-61, 764.

51. Quoted by G. Douglas Atkins, "Geoffrey H. Hartman," in *Modern American Critics*, 139, 148.

52. Ibid., 142.

53. Berman, *From the New Criticism*, 256; Hartman quoted by Berman, 255.

54. Quoted by Atkins, "Geoffrey H. Hartman," 141.

55. Hartman, "Monsieur Texte," 783-84, 789.

56. Hartman quoted by Atkins, "Geoffrey H. Hartman," 147-48.

57. Sprinker, "Aesthetic Criticism," 60-61.

58. Miller, "J. Hillis Miller on Literary Criticism," 33.

59. Harold Bloom, *The Anxiety of Influence: A Theory of Poetry* (New York: Oxford University Press, 1975), 12-13.

60. Ibid., 272, 267.

61. Helen Regueiro Elam, "Harold Bloom," in *Modern American Critics*, 38.

62. Norris, *Deconstruction*, 22

63. Christopher Norris, *Paul de Man: Deconstruction and the Critique of Aesthetic Ideology* (New York: Routledge, 1988), 2-7.

64. Lentricchia, *After the New Criticism*, 169, 184-86. The quotation is on 186.

Chapter Three

1. John Patrick Diggins, *The Rise and Fall of the American Left* (New York: W.W. Norton & Company, 1992), 279-306.

2. Martin Jay, *Marxism and Totality: The Adventures of a Concept from Lukács to Habermas* (Berkeley and Los Angeles: University of California Press, 1984), 7-9, 11-12.

3. Eugene Genovese, *In Red and Black: Marxian Explorations in Southern and Afro-American History* (New York: Pantheon Books, 1971), 391-92. The essay "On Antonio Gramsci" first appeared in 1967.

4. Raymond Williams, *Marxism and Literature* (Oxford: Oxford University Press, 1977), 19, 34; Leszek Kolakowski, *Main Currents of Marxism*, vol. 3, *The Breakdown* (New York: Oxford University Press, 1978), 242.

5. Jay, *Marxism and Totality,* 165.

6. Genovese, *In Red and Black,* 406-7.

7. Peter W. Bardaglio, "Power and Ideology in the Slave South: Eugene Genovese and His Critics," *The Maryland Historian* 12 (Fall 1981):24-25; Eugene D. Genovese, *Roll, Jordan, Roll: The World the Slaves Made* (New York: Pantheon Books, 1974), 12-22, 123-33, 365-88, 161-284, 431-41, 536-49.

8. Aptheker quoted in Peter Novick, *That Noble Dream: The "Objectivity Question" and the Historical Profession* (Cambridge: Cambridge University Press, 1988), 426n.

9. Elizabeth Fox-Genovese and Eugene D. Genovese, "The Political Crisis of Social History: A Marxian Perspective," *Journal of Social History* 10 (Winter 1976):209, 212-13.

10. Ibid., 213-15.

11. Novick, *That Noble Dream,* 434-37.

12. Genovese, *In Red and Black,* 10-12, 416, 418.

13. Raymond Williams, *Marxism and Literature* (Oxford: Oxford University Press, 1977), 163.

14. Paul A. Bovi, "The Ineluctability of Difference: Scientific Pluralism and the Critical Intelligence," in *Postmodernism and Politics,* ed. Jonathan Arac (Minneapolis: University of Minnesota Press, 1986), 5.

15. Williams, *Marxism and Literature,* 193; Terry Eagleton, *Marxism and Literary Criticism* (Berkeley and Los Angeles: University of California Press, 1976), 59-60; see also Art Berman, *From the New Criticism: The Reception of Structuralism and Poststructuralism* (Urbana: University of Illinois Press, 1988), 163.

16. Frederick Crews, *Out of My System: Psychoanalysis, Ideology, and Critical Method* (New York: Oxford University Press, 1975), 109-15.

17. Ibid., 117-18.

18. Vincent B. Leitch, *American Literary Criticism: From the Thirties to the Eighties* (New York: Columbia University Press, 1988), 371-72.

19. Louis Kampf, " 'It's Alright, Ma (I'm Only Bleeding)': Literature and Language in the Academy," *PMLA* 87 (1972):379-82.

20. Leitch, *American Literary Criticism,* 372-73.

21. Fredric Jameson, *Marxism and Form: Twentieth-Century Dialectical Theories of Literature* (Princeton: Princeton University Press, 1971), 367-68; idem, *The Prison-House of Language: A Critical Account of Structuralism and Russian Formalism* (Princeton: Princeton University Press, 1972), 23-24.

22. Jameson, *Marxism and Form,* 308-75. The quotation is on p. 308.

23. Ibid., 306.

24. Ibid., 342.

25. Jay, *Marxism and Totality,* 514-15. For an interesting and candid account of the postmodernism vs. Marxism phenomenon, see Perry Anderson, *In the Tracks of Historical Materialism* (Chicago: University of Chicago Press, 1984).

26. Alan Sheridan, *Michel Foucault: The Will to Truth* (London: Tavistock Publications, 1980), 219; Barry Smart, *Foucault, Marxism, and Critique* (London: Routledge and Keagan Paul, 1983), 89-90.

27. Sheridan, *Michel Foucault,* 219.

28. Michel Foucault quoted in Sheridan, *Michel Foucault,* 70.

29. William C. Dowling, *Jameson, Althusser, Marx: An Introduction to The Political Unconscious* (Ithaca: Cornell University Press), 50.

30. Edward Said, *Orientalism* (1978; New York: Random House, 1994), 7.

31. Ibid., 3.

32. Ibid., 3, 36, 41, 81.

33. Ibid., 12.

34. Ibid., 21.

35. Ibid., 67, 86-87, 92.

36. Thomas M. Greene, "One World, Divisible," *Yale Review* 68 (1979):577-81; Fedwa Malti-Douglas, "Re-Orienting Orientalism," *Virginia Quarterly Review* 76 (1979):724-33; J. H. Plumb, review of *Orientalism,* by Edward Said, *New York Times Book Review,* 18 February 1979.

37. Fredric Jameson, *The Political Unconscious: Narrative as a Socially Symbolic Act* (Ithaca: Cornell University Press, 1981), 62-64.

38. Ibid., 89-90.

39. Dennis Donogho, "Fredric Jameson," in *Modern American Critics: Since 1955,* ed. Gregory S. Jay (Detroit: Gale Research, 1988), 183.

40. Gerald Graff, *Literature Against Itself: Literary Ideas in Modern Society* (Chicago: University of Chicago Press, 1979), 63.

41. Ibid., 25.

42. Ibid., 8.

43. Ibid., 9.

44. Ibid., 26, 27.

45. Ibid., 119. For a leftist critique of Graff's book, see Michael Sprinker, "Criticism as Reaction," *Diacritics,* 10-11 (September 1980), 2-14.

Chapter Four

1. Brian O'Doherty, "A New Conservatism in the Seventies?" *Art in America* 59 (March-April, 1971):23.

2. See Robert Atkins, *Artspeak: A Guide to Contemporary Ideas, Movements, and Buzzwords* (New York: Abbeville Press, 1990), and Edward Lucie-Smith, *Art in the Seventies* (Ithaca: Cornell University Press, 1980).

3. Lucie-Smith, *Art in the Seventies,* 7-9.

4. Kim Levin, *Beyond Modernism: Essays on Art from the '70s and '80s* (New York: Harper and Row, 1988), xiii.

5. Atkins, *Artspeak,* 50, 69.

6. Ibid., 75-76.

7. Levin, *Beyond Modernism,* xiii.

8. Ibid., 3-4, 26; Atkins, *Artspeak,* 38.

9. Lucie-Smith, *Art in the Seventies,* 36.

10. Levin, *Beyond Modernism*, 29.

11. Suzi Gablik, "Art Under the Dollar Sign," *Art in America* 69 (December 1981):13.

12. Louis K. Meisel, *Photo-Realism* (New York: Abradale Press, 1989), 108-9.

13. Lucie-Smith, *Art in the Seventies*, 65; Atkins, *Artspeak*, 124.

14. Lucie-Smith, *Art in the Seventies*, 66.

15. Diana Crane, *The Transformation of the Avant-Garde: The New York Art World, 1940-1985* (Chicago: University of Chicago Press, 1987), 105; Henry M. Sayre, *The Object of Performance: The American Avant-Garde Since 1970* (Chicago: University of Chicago Press, 1989), 10.

16. Quoted in Lucie-Smith, *Art in the Seventies*, 68.

17. Robert Storr, "Rackstraw Downes: Painter as Geographer," *Art in America* 72 (October 1984):154-60.

18. Meisel, *Photo-Realism*, 241-42.

19. "The Photo-Realists: 12 Interviews," *Art in America* 60 (November-December 1972):74; Meisel, *Photo-Realism*, 27.

20. Quoted in Meisel, *Photo-Realism*, 177.

21. "12 Interviews," 77.

22. Quoted in Meisel, *Photo-Realism*, 27.

23. Quoted by April Kingsley in *The Turning Point: The Abstract Expressionists and the Transformation of American Art* (New York: Simon & Schuster, 1992), 38.

24. Crane, *Transformation of the Avant-Garde*, 60-61.

25. Atkins, *Artspeak*, 120-21; Lucie-Smith, *Painting in the 1970s*, 44.

26. See Budd Hopkins, "Frank Stella's New Work: A Personal Note," *Artforum* 15 (December 1976):58-59.

27. Lucie-Smith, *Art in the Seventies*, 44.

28. John Perreault, "Issues in Pattern Painting," *Artforum* 16 (November 1977):33.

29. Ibid., 33; Lucie-Smith, *Painting in the 1970s*, 47.

30. Jeanne Siegel, *Artwords: Discourse on the 60s and 70s* (New York: Da Capo Press, 1985), 101.

31. Therese Schwartz, "The Politicalization of the Avant-Garde, I," *Art in America*, 59 (November-December 1971):100; idem, "The Politicalization of the Avant-Garde, IV," *Art in America* 62 (January-February 1974): 81-82; Takis quoted in Siegel, *Artwords*, 121.

32. Quoted in Siegel, *Artwords*, 132.

33. Andre quoted in ibid., 130.

34. Quoted in Lucy Lippard, "The Art Workers' Coalition," *Idea Art*, ed. Gregory Battock (New York: Dutton, 1973), 103.

35. Henry M. Sayre, *The Object of Performance: The American Avant-Garde Since 1970* (Chicago: University of Chicago Press, 1989), 8-9. The terms "avant-garde" and "modernism" may be confusing. Generally "avant-garde" has signified a politically charged, insurgent art, with antiestablishment manifestations. Modernism might also reflect those characteristics, but it often means an art form concerned with the strictly formal aspects of art. It appears to that extent apolitical. See Andreas Huyssen, "The Search for Tradition: Avant-Garde and Postmodernism in the 1970s," *New German Critique*, No. 22 (Winter 1981):26-27.

36. Owens quoted in Sayre, *Object of Performance*, 96; Siegel, *Artwords*, 7, 13-14.

37. Siegel, *Artwords*, 6; Atkins, *Artspeak*, 76-77. See also Lawrence Alloway, "Women's Art in the '70s," *Art in America* 64 (May-June, 1976):64-68.

38. See the account by Sayre, *Object of Performance*, 145-73.

39. Ibid., 92-96; Lucie-Smith, *Painting in the 1970s*, 93-94.

40. Siegel, *Artwords*, 73; Therese Schwartz, "The Politicalization of the Avant-Garde, II," *Art in America* 60 (March-April 1971):75-76.

41. Schwartz, "Avant-Garde, II," 76.

42. See, for example, Henri Ghent, "Black Creativity in Quest of an Audience," *Art in America* 58 (May-June 1970):35.

43. Barbara Rose, "Black Art in America," *Art in America* 58 (September-October 1970):54. For more on radical art movements in the middle of the 1970s, see Nancy Marmer, "Art and Politics, '77," *Art in America* 65 (July-August 1977):64-66.

44. Douglas Davis, *Artculture: Essays on the Post-Modern* (New York: Harper & Row, 1977), 1.

45. Quoted in Schwartz, "Politicalization of the Avant-Garde, I" 97.

46. Quoted in Schwartz, "Politicalization of the Avant-Garde, II," 73.

47. Quoted ibid., 71.

48. Levin, *Beyond Modernism*, 32.

49. Quoted in Crane, *Transformation of the Avant-Garde*, 96.

50. Ibid., 3, 7, 9-11, 58.

51. Donald B. Kuspit, "Modern Art's Failure of Critical Nerve," *Arts Magazine* 53 (February 1979):116.

52. Ibid., 116-17.

53. Gablik, "Art Under the Dollar Sign," 13-19.

54. Corinne Robins, "Late Decorative Art: Art, Artifact, and the Ersatz," *Arts*, 35 (September 1980):150-51.

55. Greenberg quoted in Sayre, *Object of Performance*, 8.

56. Richard Pousette-Dart quoted in Kingsley, *The Turning Point*, 107-8, 138-39.

57. Quoted ibid., 354.

58. Quoted ibid., 35.

59. Jonathan Harris, "Modernism and Culture in the USA, 1930–1960," in *Modernism in Dispute: Art Since the Forties*, Harris et. al. contributors (New Haven: Yale University Press, 1993), 32–38.

60. Andreas Huyssen, "Mapping the Postmodern," *New German Critique* No. 33 (Fall 1984):18-27.

61. Crane, *Transformation of the Avant-Garde*, 64, 68; Christin J. Mamiya, *Pop Art and Consumer Culture: American Super Market* (Austin: University of Texas Press, 1992), 12-13.

62. Crane, *Transformation of the Avant-Garde*, 68.

63. Quoted by Mamiya, *Pop Art and Consumer Culture*, 153.

64. Mamiya, *Pop Art*, summarizing and quoting Margaret J. King, 119-20.

65. Ibid., 120, 133.

66. Hilton Kramer, *The Revenge of the Philistines: Art and Culture, 1972-1984* (New York: Free Press, 1984), 18, 6; idem, *The Age of the Avant-Garde: An Art Chronicle of 1956-1972* (New York: Farrar, Strauss, and Giroux, 1973), 526. For an extended discussion of Kramer, see my *Watch on the Right: Conservative Intellectuals in the Reagan Era* (Madison: University of Wisconsin Press, 1991), 115-42.

67. Kramer, *Age of the Avant-Garde*, 4-6.

68. Ibid., 11-13.

69. Ibid., 2-3, 15-16. For an interpretation similar to this one, see Davis, "The Avant Garde is Dead!"

70. Kramer, *Revenge of the Philistines*, 340; idem, *Age of the Avant-Garde*, 527.

71. Kramer, *Revenge of the Philistines*, 16-18.

72. Daniel Bell, *The Cultural Contradictions of Capitalism* (1976; New York: Basic Books, 1978), 7.

73. Ibid., 16-17.

74. Ibid., 17-18.

75. Ibid., 108-10.

76. Ibid., 33-35.

77. Daniel Bell, "The Revolt Against Modernity," *The Public Interest* No. 8 (Fall 1985):42-63.

78. Bell, *Cultural Contradictions of Capitalism*, 20-21, 40-41.

79. Tom Wolfe, "The Painted Word," *Harper's Magazine* 250 (April 1975):68.

80. Bell, *Cultural Contradictions of Capitalism*, 52.

Chapter Five

1. Martin Pawley, "Learning from the Rear," review of *Learning from Las Vegas*, by Robert Venturi et al., *Architectural Design*, 40 (January 1970):45.

2. Magali Sarfatti Larson, *Behind the Postmodern Facade: Architectural Change in Late Twentieth-Century America* (Berkeley and Los Angeles: University of California Press, 1993), 91-93.

3. David Harvey, *The Condition of Postmodernity* (Oxford: Basil Blackwell, 1989), 91, quoted in Larson, *Behind the Postmodern Facade*, 83-84.

4. Beverly Russell, *Architecture and Design, 1970-1990: New Ideas in America* (New York: Harry N. Abrams, 1989), 18-19, 79.

5. Robert Bruegmann, "Utilitas, Firmitas, Venustas and the Vox Populi: A Context for Controversy," in *The Critical Edge: Controversy in Recent American Architecture*, ed. Tod A. Marder (Cambridge, Mass.: MIT Press, 1985), 21.

6. Russell, *Architecture and Design*, 67-71; Ada Louise Huxtable, *Kicked A Building Lately?* (New York: Quadrangle, 1976), 56-58.

7. Russell, *Architecture and Design*, 74.

8. Tod A. Marder, "Gehry House," in *The Critical Edge*, 100-112.

9. Maria Pallerano, "Governor Nelson A. Rockefeller Empire State Plaza," in *The Critical Edge*, 87-88.

10. Ibid., 92-93.

11. Ibid., 94-96.

12. Charles Moore, in *Conversations with Architects*, ed. John W. Cook and Heinrich Klotz (New York: Praeger, 1973), 244.

13. Pallerano, "Empire State Plaza," 96.

14. M. Williams, "Facelift for Detroit," *Saturday Review*, May 14, 1977, 6.

15. Rachel B. Mullen, "Renaissance Center," in *The Critical Edge*, 176.

16. Ibid., 182; Huxtable, *Kicked A Building?*, 161-62.

17. "Architect/Developer John Portman," interview with editors of *The Journal of the Royal Institute of British Architects* 84 (December 1977):505-8.

18. Williams, "Renaissance Center," 8.

19. Robert McCabe, quoted ibid., 9.

20. Ibid., 178-79.

21. G. Conway, "The Case Against Urban Dinosaurs," *Saturday Review,* May 5, 1977, 14-15.

22. Philip Johnson, quoted in *The Critical Edge,* 182. This book offers discussions of significant buildings of the 1970s and 1980s by individual reviewers and provides comprehensive summaries of the critical assessments of them.

23. Ulrich Conrads, ed., *Programs and Manifestoes on 20th-Century Architecture,* trans. Michael Bullock (Cambridge, Mass.: MIT Press, 1964), 46.

24. Ibid., 49.

25. Ibid., 89.

26. Huxtable, *Kicked A Building?,* 61.

27. Russell, *Architecture and Design,* 23.

28. Michael Sorkin, quoted in Larson, *Behind the Postmodern Facade,* 49.

29. Leland M. Roth, *A Concise History of American Architecture* (New York: Harper and Row, 1980), 277, 284.

30. Tom Wolfe, *From Bauhaus to Our House* (New York: Farrar Strauss Giroux, 1981), 10, 24-25, 68.

31. Huxtable, *Kicked A Building?,* 45, 65.

32. George McCue, "$57,000,000 Later," *Architectural Forum* 138 (May 1973): 42-45; Russell, *Architecture and Design,* 23; Wolfe, *From Bauhaus to Our House,* 81.

33. Paul Goldberger, "Less is More—Mies Van Der Rohe; Less is a Bore—Robert Venturi," *New York Times Magazine,* October 17, 1971, 36.

34. Robert Venturi, *Complexity and Contradiction in Architecture* (1967; New York: Museum of Modern Art, 1977), 16.

35. Ibid., 41, 17.

36. Ibid., 19.

37. Ibid., 43.

38. *Conversations with Architects,* 237-38.

39. Ellen Perry Berkeley, "Mathematics at Yale," *Architectural Forum* 133 (July-August 1970):64-65.

40. "Letters," *Architectural Forum* 153 (October 1970):65.

41. Goldberger, "Less is More," 35.

42. Robert Venturi, Denise Scott Brown, and Steven Izenour, *Learning from Las Vegas: The Forgotten Symbolism of Architectural Form* (Cambridge, Mass.: MIT Press, 1977), 3, 7.

43. Ibid., 13.

44. Ibid., 13, 106-14.

45. Ibid., 153.

46. Goldberger, "Less is More," 34.

47. John Blanton, review of *Learning from Las Vegas,* by Robert Venturi, Denise Scott Brown, and Steven Izenour, *Journal of the Institute of American Architects* (January 1973):56.

48. John Cook, "Ugly is Beautiful: The Main Street School of Architecture," [Interview with Robert Venturi and Denise Scott Brown], *Atlantic,* 231 (April 1973):38.

49. Goldberger, "Less is More," 104.

50. Cook, "Ugly is Beautiful," 37.

51. Denise Scott Brown, "Learning from Pop," *Journal of Popular Culture* 7 (1973): 390-91; Goldberger quoting Brown, in "Less is More," 104.

52. Paul Goldberger, "Philip Johnson at 70: Enfant Terrible and Elder States-man," *Artnews* 75 (Summer 1976):127; Philip Johnson, "Re Building," *New York Times*, December 28, 1978, A-17.

53. Paul Golberger, "A Major Monument of Postmodernism," *New York Times*, March 31, 1978, B-4.

54. Quoted in Gregory Gilbert, "AT&T Corporate Headquarters," in *The Critical Edge*, 58.

55. Quoted ibid., 48.

56. Goldberger, "Major Monument," B-4.

57. Charles Jencks, *The Language of Post-Modern Architecture* (New York: Razzoli, 1977), 131; see also idem, "Late Modernism and Post Modernism," *Architectural Design* 48 (1978):600.

58. Gilbert, "AT&T Headquarters," 51.

59. Philip Johnson, quoted ibid., 49.

60. [Philip Johnson], "Two Current Projects: (a discussion)," *Architectural Record*, 164 (July 1978):87.

61. Ibid., 85; Goldberger, "Johnson at 70," 129; [Johnson], "Current Projects," 89; Philip Johnson, *Conversations with Architects*, 36-37.

62. Johnson, "Re Building," A-17; [Johnson], "Current Projects," 85.

63. Johnson, "Re Building," A-17.

64. Paul Goldberger, "Architecture Works of Michael Graves," *New York Times*, May 11, 1979, C-21.

65. Michael Graves, "A Case for Figurative Architecture," in *Michael Graves: Build-ings and Projects, 1966-1981*, ed. Karen Vogel Wheeler et. al. (New York: Rizzoli, 1982), 11-13.

66. Vincent Scully, "Michael Graves' Allusive Architecture: The Problem of Mass," in *Michael Graves: Buildings and Projects*, 293-94.

67. David L. Gilbert, "The Portland Building," in *The Critical Edge*, 163.

68. Ibid., 163.

69. Gilbert, "Portland Building," 165-66.

Chapter Six

1. For a general history of the woman's movement in the 1970s, see Winifred D. Wandersee, *On the Move: American Women in the 1970s* (Boston: Twayne Publishers, 1988).

2. Ibid., 1-15.

3. See, for example, Jane Alpert, "Forum: Mother Right—A New Feminist The-ory," *Ms.*, 2 (August 1973):53-55+.

4. See, for example, *The Impact of Feminist Research in the Academy*, ed. Christie Farnham (Bloomington: Indiana University Press, 1987), which has essays on anthro-pology, history, religious studies, psychology, science, sociology, and other topics.

5. For a useful overview of feminist thought, see Rosemarie Tong, *Feminist Thought: A Comprehensive Introduction* (Boulder, Co.: Westview Press, 1989).

6. Kate Millett, *Sexual Politics* (Garden City, N.Y.: Doubleday, 1970), 31-33.

7. Ibid., 31.

8. Ellen Moers, *Literary Women* (New York: Doubleday, 1976), 62-63.

9. Ibid., 60-61.

10. Elaine Showalter, *A Literature of Their Own: British Women Novelists from Brontë to Lessing* (Princeton: Princeton University Press, 1977), 5.

11. Ibid., 6-7.

12. Ibid., 12.

13. Ibid., 13.

14. Sandra M. Gilbert and Susan Gubar, *The Madwoman in the Attic: The Woman Writer and the Nineteenth-Century Literary Imagination* (New Haven: Yale University Press, 1979), 4-6, 1. The major women writers studied in this book are Jane Austen, Charlotte Brontë, Emily Brontë, Mary Shelley, and Emily Dickinson.

15. Ibid., 13.

16. The classic feminist account of this double imagery is Simone de Beauvoir's *The Second Sex* (1953).

17. Gilbert and Gubar, *Madwoman*, 45-51.

18. Ibid., 45-59.

19. Ibid., 72.

20. Ibid., 73-79. Gilbert and Gubar in this part of their book were able to draw on other American feminist theorists who also approached the female subject obliquely. Especially significant is Patricia Ann Meyer Spacks, *The Female Imagination* (New York: Knopf, 1975).

21. Art Berman, *From the New Criticism to Deconstruction: The Reception of Structuralism and Poststructuralism* (Urbana: University of Illinois Press, 1988), 185-94; Toril Moi, *Sexual/Textual Politics: Feminist Literary Theory* (London: Methuen, 1985), 99-101; Janet Todd, *Feminist Literary History* (New York: Routledge, 1988), 52-53.

22. Jane Gallop, *Thinking Through the Body* (New York: Columbia University Press, 1988), 126.

23. Rosalind Jones, "Inscribing Femininity: French Theories of the Feminine," in *Making a Difference: Feminist Literary Theory*, ed. Gayle Greene and Coppelia Kahn (London: Methuen, 1985), 83.

24. See Todd, *Feminist Literary Theory*, 38-39.

25. Nelly Furman, "The Politics of Language: Beyond the Gender Principle," in *Making a Difference*, 71, 74.

26. Elaine Marks, "Women and Literature in France," *Signs* 3 (1978):833.

27. Hilene Cixous, "The Laugh of the Medusa," *Signs* 1 (1976):883.

28. Ibid., 879.

29. Marks, "Women and Literature in France," 836.

30. Ibid., 836; Carolyn Greenstein Burke, "Report from Paris: Women's Writing and the Women's Movement," *Signs* 3 (Summer 1978):845.

31. Marks, "Women and Literature in France," 837.

32. Ibid, 838; Burke, "Report from France," 849.

33. Marks, "Women and Literature in France," 848-49; Burke, "Report from France," 846, 840-41.

34. Cixous quoted by Jones in *Making a Difference*, 85.

35. Millett, *Sexual Politics*, 176-220.

36. Moi, *Sexual/Textual Politics*, 26, 30.

37. Ibid., 6-8.

38. Moi, *Sexual/Textual Politics*, 61, 63.

39. Ibid., 61-67; Gilbert and Gubar, *Madwoman*, 101; see also Mary Jacobus, review of *Madwoman in the Attic*, *Signs* 6 (Spring, 1981):517-23.

40. Gayle Greene and Coppelia Kahn, "Feminist Scholarship and the Social Construction of Women," in *Making a Difference,* 25-26.

41. Elaine Showalter, "Towards a Feminist Poetics," in *Women Writing and Writing About Women,* ed. Mary Jacobus (London: Croom Helm, 1979, 1985), 38.

42. Ibid., 38-39.

43. See for example, Gerda Lerner, *The Majority Finds Its Past: Placing Women in History* (Oxford: Oxford University Press, 1979), 173, 179.

44. Sheila Ryan Johansson, "'Herstory'" As History: A New Field or Another Fad?" in *Liberating Women's History: Theoretical and Critical Essays,* ed. Berenice A. Carroll (Urbana: University of Illinois Press, 1976), 400.

45. Peter Novick, *That Noble Dream: The "Objectivity Question" and the American Historical Profession* (Cambridge: Cambridge University Press), 494, 496.

46. Ann D. Gordon, Mari Jo Buhle, and Nancy Schrom Dye, "The Problem of Women's History," in *Liberating Women's History,* 75.

47. Linda Gordon et al., "Historical Phallacies: Sexism in American Historical Writing," in *Liberating Women's History,* 57, 59.

48. Gerda Lerner, "Placing Women in History: A 1975 Perspective," in *Liberating Women's History,* 358-59.

49. Hilda Smith, "Feminism and Methodology in Women's History," in *Liberating Women's History,* 369-71.

50. Lerner, "Placing Women in History," 352-53.

51. Ann D. Gordon, Mari Jo Buhle, and Nancy Schrom Dye, "The Problem of Women's History," 86-87.

52. Ibid., 87.

53. Ellen DuBois, "The Radicalism of the Women's Suffrage Movement: Notes Toward the Reconstruction of Nineteenth-Century Feminism," *Feminist Studies* 3 (1975-1976), 64.

54. Ibid., 65.

55. Ibid., 64-65; idem, contribution to "Politics and Culture in Women's History," forum in *Feminist Studies* 6 (1980):31.

56. Of particular importance here are Nancy F. Cott, *The Bonds of Womanhood: "Women's Sphere" in New England, 1780-1835* (New Haven: Yale University Press, 1977); Kathryn Kish Sklar *Catherine Beecher: A Study in American Domesticity* (New Haven: Yale University Press, 1973); Carroll Smith-Rosenberg, "The Female World of Love and Ritual: Relations Between Women in Nineteenth-Century America," *Signs* 1 (Autumn 1975), 1-29.

57. Carroll Smith-Rosenberg, in "Politics and Culture in Women's History: A Symposium" *Feminist Studies* 6 (1980):55-58; idem, "The New Woman and the New History," *Feminist Studies* 3 (1975-1976), 185-86, 188.

58. Smith-Rosenberg, "Symposium" *Feminist Studies* 6 (1980):62.

59. Mari Jo Buhle, "Symposium" *Feminist Studies* 6 (1980):39-41.

Chapter Seven

1. Ron Karenga quoted in John Runcie, "The Black Culture Movement and the Black Community," *American Studies* 10 (1976):197.

2. William L. Van Deburg, *New Day in Babylon: The Black Power Movement and American Culture, 1965-1975* (Chicago: University of Chicago Press, 1992), 248-58.

3. Ron Karenga, "Black Cultural Nationalism," in *The Black Aesthetic,* ed. Addison Gayle, Jr. (New York: Doubleday, 1971), 31-36.

4. John Oliver Killens quoted in Francis and Val Gray Ward, "The Black Artist: His Role in the Struggle," *The Black Scholar* (January 1971):29; see also, Bernard W. Bell, *The Afro-American Novel and Its Tradition* (Amherst, Mass.: University of Massachusetts Press, 1987), 245-53.

5. Hoyt W. Fuller, "Towards a Black Aesthetic," in *The Black Aesthetic*, 3, 7-9; see also Addison Gayle, Jr., "Black Literature and the White Aesthetic," in *The Black Aesthetic*, 43.

6. Barbara Rose, "Black Art in America," *Art in America* 58 (September-October, 1970):54.

7. Darwin T. Turner, "Afro-American Literary Criticism: An Introduction," in *The Black Aesthetic*, 71-73.

8. See Henri Ghent, "Black Creativity in Quest of an Audience," *Art in America* 58 (May-June 1970):35.

9. Peter Novick, *That Noble Dream: The "Objectivity Question" and the American Historical Profession* (New York: Cambridge University Press, 1988), 475-76.

10. Ibid., 484-85. See also the major works in question here: Lawrence Levine, *Black Culture and Black Consciousness* (New York: Oxford University Press, 1977); George R. Rawick, *From Sundown to Sunup: The Making of a Black Community* (Westport, Conn.: Greenwood Press, 1972); Herbert Gutman, *The Black Family in Slavery and Freedom* (New York: Pantheon Books, 1974).

11. John Runcie, "Black Culture Movement," 190, 193; Robert Weisbord, *Ebony Kinship: Africa, Africans, and the Afro-American* (Westport, Conn.: Greenwood Press, 1973), 193-94.

12. Weisbord, *Ebony Kinship*, 188-89.

13. Sheila Walker, "Black English," *Black World* 20 (June 1971):4-7.

14. J. L. Dillard, *Black English: Its History and Usage in the United States* (New York: Vintage Books, 1972), 5-7, 115-23.

15. Weisbord, *Ebony Kinship*, 201.

16. Ron Karenga, "A Strategy for Struggle," *Black Scholar* 5 (November 1973):9, 13.

17. Maulana Ron Karenga, "Ideology and Struggle: Some Preliminary Notes," *Black Scholar* 6 (January-February 1975):24.

18. Ibid., 25-26.

19. Runcie, "Black Culture Movement," 205-6.

20. Ibid., 207-8.

21. Francis and Val Gray Ward, "The Black Artist—His Role in the Struggle," *Black Scholar* 2 (January 1971):26.

22. Runcie, "Black Culture Movement," 209-10.

23. Ralph Ellison, "Romare Bearden: Paintings and Projections," *The Crisis* 77 (March 1970): 81-86.

24. Ibid., 84.

25. Ibid., 84, 86.

26. Bayard Rustin, "The Role of the Artist in the Freedom Struggle," *The Crisis* 77 (August-September 1970):260-61.

27. Ibid., 261.

28. Houston Baker, Jr., *The Journey Back: Issues in Black Literature and Criticism* (Chicago: University of Chicago Press, 1980), 134, xi.

29. Ibid., xii.

30. Houston Baker cited key American texts on structuralism: Robert Scholes' *Structuralism in Literature* (1976), Jonathan Culler's *Structuralist Poetics* (1975), and Terence Hawkes' *Structuralism and Semiotics* (1977). See Baker, *The Journey Back*, 6, 170.

31. Baker, *The Journey Back*, xiv.

32. Ibid., 20-21, 31-32.

33. Ibid., 33.

34. Ibid., 36-38.

35. Ibid., 43.

36. Ibid., 157-59.

37. In Black literary criticism, for example, see Houston Baker, Jr., *Blues, Ideology, and Afro-American Literature: A Vernacular Theory* (Chicago: University of Chicago Press, 1984), and Henry Louis Gates, *The Signifying Monkey: A Theory of Afro-American Literary Criticism* (New York: Oxford University Press), 1988.

38. Michele Wallace, *Black Macho and the Myth of the Superwoman* (New York: Dial Press, 1978), 6-7, 162.

39. Ibid., 24.

40. Ibid., 30, 48.

41. Ibid., 39-41, 49.

42. Ibid., 91-93, 122, 127.

43. Sarah Webster Fabio, "Blowing the Whistle on Some Jive," *Black Scholar* 10 (May-June 1979):58. One of many short contributions to a feature forum on black male/female relations.

44. Sherely A. Williams, "Comment on the Curb," in *Black Scholar* 10 (May-June 1979):50.

45. Pauline Terrelonge Stone, "The Limitations of Reformist Feminism," in *Black Scholar* 10 (May-June 1979):24.

46. Terry Jones, "The Need to Go Beyond Stereotypes," *Black Scholar* 10 (May-June 1979):48.

47. Askia M. Toure, "Black/Female Relations: A Political Overview of the 1970s," in *Black Scholar* 10 (May-June 1979):47.

48. June Jordan, "To Be Black and Female," review of Michele Wallace, *Black Macho and the Myth of the Superwoman, New York Times Book Review,* March 18, 1979, 15, 35.

49. Bell, *Afro-American Novel*, 259-65.

50. Barbara A. Sizemore, "Sexism and the Black Male," *Black Scholar* 4 (March-April 1973):6-8.

51. Angela Davis, *An Autobiography* (New York: Random House, 1974), 161.

52. Elizabeth F. Hood, "Black Women, White Women: Separate Paths to Liberation," *Black Scholar* 9 (April 1978):47, 50-53.

53. Angela Davis, "Rape, Racism, and the Capitalist Setting," *Black Scholar* 9 (April 1978):27-30.

54. Robert Staples, "The Myth of Black Macho: A Response to Angry Black Feminists," *Black Scholar* 10 (March-April 1979):25, 28.

55. Ibid., 31.

56. Stone, "Limitations of Reformist Feminism," 25-27.

57. Julianne Malveaux, "The Sexual Politics of Black People: Angry Black Women, Angry Black Men," in *Black Scholar* 10 (May-June 1979):32.

58. Toure, "Black Male/Female Relations," 47.

59. Audre Lorde, "The Great American Disease," in *Black Scholar* forum, 17, 19.

60. Alvin F. Poussaint, "White Manipulation and Black Oppression," *Black Scholar* 10 (May-June 1979):53-55. A more complete review of Poussaint's essay would note

that he also saw a counter image of the black male, that of the shuffling, shiftless, and passive "boy."

Chapter Eight

1. Quoted in William B. Hixson, Jr., *Search for the American Right Wing: An Analysis of the Social Science Record, 1955-1957* (Princeton: Princeton University Press, 1992), 5.

2. Ibid., 11-12, 17-18.

3. Ibid., 19, 27-29, 41-42.

4. George Wallace quoted in Richard M. Scammon and Ben J. Wattenberg, *The Real Majority* (1970; New York: Primus, 1992), 62.

5. Thomas F. Petigrew, *Racially Separate or Together* (New York: McGraw-Hill, 1971), 236-56.

6. Hixson, *Search for the American Right Wing*, 122-23. See also Dan T. Carter, *The Politics of Rage: George Wallace, the Origins of the New Conservatism and the Transformation of American Politics* (New York: Simon & Schuster, 1995), 324-70.

7. Kevin P. Phillips, *The Emerging Republican Majority* (New Rochelle, N.Y.: Arlington House, 1969), 40.

8. Ibid., 84.

9. Ibid., 44, 88.

10. Jerome L. Himmelstein, *To the Right: The Transformation of American Conservatism* (Berkeley and Los Angeles: University of California Press, 1990), 97-128.

11. See Jeffrey K. Hadden and Charles E. Swann, *Prime-Time Preachers: The Rising Power of Televangelism* (New York: Addison-Wesley, 1981).

12. That trend had begun in the 1960s. For an analysis, see Dean M. Kelley, *Why Conservative Churches Are Growing: A Study in the Sociology of Religion* (New York: Harper & Row, 1972).

13. Among this literature, see especially Paul Kleppner, *The Cross of Culture: A Social Analysis of Midwestern Politics, 1850-1900* (New York: Free Press, 1970); Richard J. Jensen, *The Winning of the Midwest: Social and Political Conflict, 1888-1896* (Chicago: University of Chicago Press, 1971); Ronald P. Formisano, *The Birth of Mass Political Parties, Michigan, 1827-1861* (Princeton: Princeton University Press, 1971); Robert Kelley, *The Cultural Pattern in American Politics: The First Century* (New York: Knopf, 1979).

14. Kevin P. Phillips, *Mediacracy: American Parties and Politics in the Communications Age* (Garden City, N.Y.: Doubleday, 1975), v.

15. Ibid., 15.

16. Ibid., 17, 26-27, 33.

17. Ibid., 21.

18. Ibid., 22, 65.

19. Ibid., 41, 57, 125-28.

20. See Sidney Blumenthal, *The Rise of the Counter-Establishment: From Conservative Ideology to Political Power* (New York: Times Books, 1986).

21. J. David Hoeveler, Jr., *Watch on the Right: Conservative Intellectuals in the Reagan Era* (Madison: University of Wisconsin Press, 1991), 1-10. This material, and the following account of neoconservatism, have been summarized from this book. See also Gary Dorrien, *The Neoconservative Mind: Politics, Culture, and the War of Ideology* (Philadelphia: Temple University Press, 1993).

22. Norman Podhoretz, *Breaking Ranks: A Political Memoir* (New York: Harper and Row, 1979), 150, 91, 284-85. Podhoretz's anticommunism had remained even throughout his "radical" years.

23. See Norman Podhoretz, *The Bloody Crossroads: Where Literature and Politics Meet* (New York: Simon & Schuster, 1986), 115-135. The "Adversary Culture" essay first appeared in 1979.

24. See Jeanne J. Kirkpatrick, "Politics and the New Class," *Society,* 16 (January-February 1979):42-48.

25. E. J. Dionne, Jr., *Why Americans Hate Politics* (New York: Simon & Schuster, 1991), 49.

26. Ibid., 123, 107.

27. Nathan Glazer, "On Being Deradicalized," *Commentary,* 50(October, 1970):74-75.

28. Ibid., 75.

29. Nathan Glazer, *Affirmative Discrimination: Ethnic Inequality and Public Policy* (1975; New York: Basic Books, 1978), 110, 200, 202-3, 219.

30. Irving Kristol, *Reflections of a Neoconservative: Looking Back, Looking Ahead* (New York: Basic Books, 1983), 12.

31. Irving Kristol, "Why I am For Humphrey," *New Republic,* 8 June 1968, 22; Walter Goodman, "Irving Kristol: Patron Saint of the New Right," *New York Times Magazine* December 6, 1981:200; Geoffrey Norman, "The Godfather of Neoconservatism (and His Family)," *Esquire* February 13, 1979:37-39.

32. Irving Kristol, "Skepticism, Meliorism, and the Public Interest," *The Public Interest* no. 81 (Fall 1985):32.

33. Irving Kristol, "When Virtue Loses All Her Loveliness—Some Reflections on Capitalism and the 'Free Society,'" *The Public Interest* no. 21 (Fall 1970):10; Irving Kristol, *Two Cheers for Capitalism* (New York: Basic Books, 1978), 28-29, 87-89.

34. Kristol, "When Virtue Loses All her Loveliness," 11.

35. Kristol, "Two Cheers for Capitalism," 166.

36. Ibid., 147.

37. Michael Novak, *The Rise of the Unmeltable Ethnics: Politics and Culture in the Seventies* (New York: Macmillan, 1972), 203.

38. Ibid., 47, 86, 126, 245-46. See also 68-71 for an elaboration of this complaint.

39. Ibid., 123.

40. Ibid., 37.

41. Ibid., 9, 249.

42. Michael Novak, *Choosing Our King: Powerful Symbols in Presidential Politics* (New Brunswick, N.J.: 1974), 70-71; Michael Novak, "Switch to Reagan for a Strong America," *Commonweal* 24 (October 1980):589.

43. Michael Novak, "A Changed View of 'The Movement,'" *Christian Century* 13 (September 1978):830.

44. Robert Nisbet, "The Dilemma of Conservatives in a Populist Society," *Policy Review* no. 4 (Spring, 1978): 92-93.

45. Robert Nisbet, *Prejudices: A Philosophical Dictionary* (Cambridge, Mass.,: Harvard University Press, 1982), 55.

46. Robert Nisbet, *Twilight of Authority* (New York: Oxford University Press, 1975), 195.

47. Ibid., 196-97.

48. Robert Nisbet, *Emile Durkheim: With Selected Essays* (1965; Westport, Conn., 1976), 3-4; see also, idem, *Twilight of Authority,* 8-9.

49. George F. Will, *The Pursuit of Virtue and Other Tory Notions* (New York: Simon & Schuster, 1982), 40; idem, *Statecraft as Soulcraft: What Government Does* (New York: Simon & Schuster, 1983), 146.

50. George F. Will, *The Pursuit of Happiness and Other Sobering Thoughts* (New York: Harper and Row, 1978), 113-14.

51. Will, *Pursuit of Virtue,* 352-54; idem, *Pursuit of Happiness,* 308.

52. Will, *Pursuit of Happiness,* 46; idem, *Pursuit of Virtue,* 31.

53. Will, *Pursuit of Happiness,* 60-61, 191; idem, *Pursuit of Virtue,* 103.

54. Will, *Statecraft as Soulcraft,* 142-43.

55. Will, *Pursuit of Happiness,* 238.

56. Will, *Pursuit of Virtue,* 242.

57. Will, *Pursuit of Happiness,* 206.

58. Ibid., 33.

59. Peter Viereck, *Conservatism Revisited* (1949; New York: The Free Press, 1962), 34-35.

60. Dionne, *Why Americans Hate Politics,* 17.

61. See Robert Bellah, et al., *Habits of the Heart: Individualism and Commitment in American Life* (New York: Harper and Row, 1985), and Arthur M. Schlesinger, Jr., *The Dismantling of America: Reflections on a Multicultural Society* (New York: Norton, 1992).

Chapter Nine

1. Elliott Abrams, in "What is a Liberal—Who is a Conservative?" [A Symposium], *Commentary* 62 (September 1976):34; Carl Gershman, *Commentary* 62 (September 1976):59.

2. Pearl K. Bell, *Commentary* 62 (September 1976):43.

3. Ibid., 43; Eric F. Goldman, in *Commentary* 62 (September 1976):63.

4. Bayard Rustin, *Commentary* 62 (September 1976):94; Gus Tyler, *Commentary* 62 (September 1976):101.

5. Roger Starr, *Commentary* 62 (September 1976):100.

6. Edith Efron, *Commentary* 62 (September 1976):51.

7. Joseph Epstein, *Commentary* 62 (September 1976):53.

8. Midge Decter, *Commentary* 62 (September 1976):50.

9. Sidney Hook, *Commentary* 62 (September 1976):69.

10. Irving Kristol, *Commentary* 62 (September 1976):74.

11. See *Reading Rawls: Critical Studies on Rawls' 'A Theory of Justice,'* ed. Norman Daniels (Stanford, Calif.: Stanford University Press, 1975).

12. John Rawls, *A Theory of Justice* (Cambridge, Mass.: Harvard University Press, 1971), 3.

13. Ibid., 22-23n.

14. Ibid., 22-25.

15. Ibid., 11.

16. Ibid., 11-13.

17. Ibid., 30-31.

18. Ibid., 60-61, 62-63.

19. Ibid., 75, 78.

20. Ibid., 64.

21. Ibid., 219.

22. Ibid., 224-39, 271-84; Chandran Kukathas and Philip Pettit, *Rawls: A Theory of Justice and Its Critics* (Stanford, Calif.: Stanford University Press, 1990), 51.

23. Rawls, *A Theory of Justice*, 255.

24. Milton Fisk, "History and Reason in Rawls' Moral Theory," in *Reading Rawls*, 59-60.

25. Ibid., 57-58.

26. Allan Bloom, *Giants and Dwarfs: Essays, 1960-1990* (New York: Simon & Schuster, 1990), 315-16. Bloom's critique first appeared in *American Political Science Review* 62 (June 1975): 648-62.

27. Bloom, *Giants and Dwarfs*, 318-19.

28. Ibid., 329-31, 342-44.

29. See George H. Nash, *The Conservative Intellectual Movement: Since 1945* (New York: Basic Books, 1976), 1-8.

30. Ibid., 313-18.

31. "As I See It: A Talk with Robert Nozick," *Forbes*, March 15, 1972:22.

32. Peter Singer, review of *Anarchy, State, and Utopia*, by Robert Nozick, *New York Review of Books*, March 6, 1975:6.

33. Robert Nozick, *Anarchy, State, and Utopia* (New York: Basic Books, 1974), 6-23, 51-53, 90-95, 113-15.

34. Ibid., 151.

35. Ibid., 159.

36. Ibid., 163.

37. Ibid., 183.

38. Ibid., 190.

39. Ibid., 195.

40. Ibid., 209, 209n.

41. Rawls had written: "Within the limits allowed by the background arrangements, distributive shares are decided by the outcome of the natural lottery; and that outcome is arbitrary from a moral perspective.... Even the willingness to make an effort, to try, and so to be deserving in the ordinary sense is itself dependent on happy family and social circumstances," *A Theory of Justice*, 74.

42. Nozick, *Anarchy, State, and Utopia*, 214.

43. Ibid., 223, 232-33.

44. Ibid., 271-72; "As I See It," 23.

45. See, for example, "As I See It," 22.

46. Ibid., 24.

Afterword

1. *The Anti-Aesthetic: Essays on Postmodern Culture*, ed. Hal Foster (Port Townsend, Wash.: Bay Press, 1983), 111-25.

2. Steven Best and Douglas Kellner, *Postmodern Theory: Critical Interrogations* (New York: Guilford Press, 1991), 146.

3. Jean-Francois Lyotard, *The Post-Modern Condition: A Report on Knowledge*, trans. Geoff Bennington and Brian Massuni (1979; Minneapolis: University of Minnesota Press, 1984), 3-5, 12, 33-37.

4. Fredric Jameson, *Postmodernism, or the Cultural Logic of Late Capitalism* (Durham, N.C.: Duke University Press, 1991), xiv, 6.

5. Ibid., 3-4.

6. Ibid., 38, 15; Fredric Jameson, "Regarding Postmodernism: A Conversation with Fredric Jameson," in *Postmodernism: Jameson: Critique*, ed. Douglas Kellner (Washington, D.C.: Maisonneuve Press, 1989), 44-45.

7. Douglas Kellner, "Jameson, Marxism, and Postmodernism," in *Postmodernism: Jameson: Critique*, 15-16, 27, 32; Fredric Jameson, *The Political Unconscious: Narrative as a Socially Symbolic Act* (Ithaca: Cornell University Press, 1981), 9.

8. Jameson, *Postmodernism*, 14-21; Jameson, "Regarding Postmodernism," 44, 60.

9. Best and Kellner, *Postmodern Theory*, 111.

10. Jean Baudrillard, *Selected Writings*, ed. Mark Poster (Stanford, Calif.: Stanford University Press, 1988), 78-79.

11. Best and Kellner, *Postmodern Theory*, 120-21.

12. David S. Gross, "Marxism and Resistance: Fredric Jameson and the Moment of Postmodernism," in *Postmodernism: Jameson: Critique*, 109-11.

13. Jameson, *Postmodernism*, 48-49; idem, "Regarding Postmodernism," 69; David S. Gross, quoting Jameson, in "Marxism and Resistance: Fredric Jameson and the Moment of Postmodernism," in *Postmodernism: Jameson: Critique*, 106.

14. Steven Best, "Jameson, Totality, and the Poststructuralist Critique," in *Postmodernism: Jameson: Critique*, 361.

15. For a close study of Rorty's philosophy and helpful bibliographical references, see David L. Hall, *Richard Rorty: Prophet and Poet of the New Pragmatism* (Albany, N.Y.: State University of New York Press, 1994).

16. Richard Rorty, *Consequences of Pragmatism: Essays: 1972-1980* (Minneapolis: University of Minnesota, 1982), 41; idem, *Philosophy and the Mirror of Nature* (Princeton: Princeton University Press, 1979), 3-4.

17. Rorty, *Philosophy and the Mirror of Nature*, 12, 131-32, 163, 249.

18. Ibid., 8-10, 165-67, 357; Rorty, *Consequences of Pragmatism*, xvi.

19. Rorty, *Consequences of Pragmatism*, 148-49.

20. Rorty, *Philosophy and the Mirror of Nature*, 162.

21. Rorty, *Consequences of Pragmatism*, 46, 49; Rorty, *Philosophy and the Mirror of Nature*, 368.

22. Rorty, *Philosophy and the Mirror of Nature*, 371.

23. Rorty, *Consequences of Pragmatism*, xx-xxi.

24. Ibid., 151-52.

25. Ibid., 150-51.

26. Rorty, *Philosophy and the Mirror of Nature*, 315-19, 325. In his reconstruction of philosophy, Rorty followed some of the directions taken by contemporary philosophers Wilfrid Sellars and W. V. O. Quine.

27. Ibid., 356; Rorty, *Consequences of Pragmatism*, xix, xvii.

28. Rorty, *Consequences of Pragmatism*, xvi-xviii.

29. Ibid., xxxix; Rorty, *Philosophy and the Mirror of Nature*, 178.

30. Ibid., 16, 45, 48-49, 51-52, 76, 86-87.

31. Johnathan Culler quoted by Charles B. Guignon and David R. Hiley, "Biting the Bullet: Rorty on Private and Public Morality," in *Reading Rorty*, ed. Alan Malachowski (Oxford: Basil Blackwell, 1990), 345.

32. Ibid., 342, 346, 352.

33. Ibid., 293; Rorty, *Consequences of Pragmatism,* 96.

34. Rorty, *Consequences of Pragmatism,* 204-5, 206-7.

35. Rorty, *Philosophy and the Mirror of Nature,* 210; Guignon and Hiley, "Biting the Bullitt"; see especially Richard Rorty, "The Contingency of Selfhood," *London Review of Books,* April 17, 1986: 11-14; idem, "The Contingency of Community," *London Review of Books,* May 8, 1986:10-14.

36. Rorty, *Consequences of Pragmatism,* 210n, 290; Guignon and Hiley, "Biting the Bullet," 340-41.

37. See Richard Rorty, "Postmodernist Bourgeois Liberalism," *Journal of Philosophy* 80 (September-October, 1983): 583-89.

Bibliographic Essay

I offer in what follows some suggestions for further reading in the subjects discussed in this book. I have not tried to duplicate the various listings in end-note references (those would be the first clues for more in-depth study), but have sought instead to direct readers to sources that will supplement the material discussed in the preceding pages. In some cases I do refer to some previously listed items, especially when these sources will provide a larger context or history.

Readers interested in a general history of the 1970s might begin with Peter N. Carroll's *It Seemed Like Nothing Happened: The Tragedy and Promise of America in the 1970s* (New York: Holt, Rinehart and Winston, 1982). An entertaining and often acute reading of the decade is offered by Andrew J. Edelstein and Kevin McDonough in their book *The Seventies: From Hot Pants to Hot Tubs* (New York: Dutton, 1990). *The Seventies* offers some nice overviews of popular culture and its running time line keeps everything in perspective. The "Seventies" section of *American Chronicle: Six Decades of American Life, 1920-1980*, ed. Lois Gordon and Alan Gordon will provide the reader a comprehensive review of the decade with an arrangement in categories such as politics, ads, movies, TV, popular music, theater, books, science and technology, sports and fashion.

On technology and the information culture, in addition to the works by Alvin Toffler, Daniel Bell, and Christopher Lasch discussed in Chapter One, see *The Myths of Information: Technology and Postindustrial Culture*, ed. Kathleen Woodward (Madison, Wis.: Coda Press, 1980). It contains essays on communication culture, mass culture, art, and cybernetics.

For the beginner in the subject, Raman Selden's *A Reader's Guide to Contemporary Literary Theory* (Lexington: University of Kentucky Press, 1985) will be

211

very helpful. It begins with Russian formalism and moves through other schools to a concluding chapter on feminist criticism. *Deconstruction: Theory and Practice* (Routledge: London, 1982) by Christopher Norris provides a mostly nontechnical introduction to this subject and includes the American reception. Jonathan Culler's *On Deconstruction: Theory and Criticism after Structuralism* (Ithaca: Cornell University Press, 1982) is more technical. There are some very helpful introductions to the history of modern literary theory. Terry Eagleton, *Literary Theory: An Introduction* (Minneapolis: University of Minnesota Press, 1983), is a very readable book, from a Marxist perspective. Those interested in Marxism will also want to look at Eagleton's *The Ideology of the Aesthetic* (Cambridge, MA: Basil Blackwell, 1990), a brilliant book, but far more technical. Art Berman, *From the New Criticism to Deconstruction: The Reception of Structuralism and Post-Structuralism* (Urbana: University of Illinois Press, 1988) covers the French and American scenes very well. Vincent B. Leitch, *American Literary Criticism: From the 30s to the 80s* (New York: Columbia University Press, 1988) begins with Marxism and the New Criticism and carries through to subjects on Black Aesthetics and feminism. Frank Lentricchia, *After the New Criticism* (Chicago: University of Chicago Press, 1980) had considerable influence and included some polemical points that showed how quickly literary theory became politicized in the United States. The subject took on renewed interest in the late 1980s with the shocking disclosure that Yale deconstructionist Paul de Man had written for the Belgian pro-Nazi publication *Le Soir* in his early years. See the engrossing report of this story by David Lehrman, *Signs of the Times: Deconstruction and the Fall of Paul de Man* (New York: Simon & Schuster, 1991). See also the collection of documents about the "case" published as *Responses: On Paul de Man's Wartime Journalism*, eds. Werner Hamacher, Neil Hertz, and Thomas Keenan (Lincoln: University of Nebraska Press, 1989). The reader may also want to look at *Against Deconstruction*, by John M. Ellis (Princeton: Princeton University Press, 1989).

On Marxism and its relation to literature, one might want to begin with a large historical setting, provided by Martin Jay's impressive study *Marxism and Totality: The Adventures of a Concept from Lukács to Habermas* (Berkeley and Los Angeles: University of California Press, 1984). In addition to the individuals in the title, the book discusses Karl Korsch, Gramsci, Ernst Bloch, Marcuse, Adorno, Maurice Merleau-Ponty, Althusser, and others. A more summary treatment is Terry Eagleton's *Marxism and Literary Criticism* (Berkeley and Los Angeles: University of California Press, 1976). See also Raymond Williams, *Marxism and Literature* (Oxford: Oxford University Press, 1977) and Tony Bennett, *Formalism and Marxism* (London: Methuen, 1979). Perry Anderson, *In the Tracks of Historical Materialism* (Chicago: University of Chicago Press, 1983) clearly shows how poststructuralism challenged Marxism in Europe.

Many readers will want to consult the several good studies of Foucault now available before they go to the original writings. *Foucault: The Will to Truth*, by

Alan Sheridan (Tavistock Publications: London, 1980) will be a helpful introduction. Barry Smart, *Foucault, Marxism, and Critique* (London: Routledge and Keagan Paul, 1983) shows why Foucault had such an impact on European Marxism. *Foucault: A Critical Reader,* edited by David Couzens Hoy (Oxford: Basil Blackwell, 1986), has fifteen essays that focus on some narrow thematic points in the Foucault corpus. In 1993 appeared the remarkable biography of Foucault by Jim Miller, *The Passion of Michel Foucault* (New York: Simon & Schuster, 1993) which discloses the bizarre aspects of Foucault's life to the heretofore unaware.

Of the several works of Fredric Jameson discussed in the book, the reader may want to pay particular attention to his major work of 1991, *Postmodernism, or the Cultural Logic of Late Capitalism* (Durham: Duke University Press, 1991). It is both an expansive look at postmodernist culture, covering subjects from architecture to film, but an intellectual document in itself, representing Marxist criticism at its most suggestive. Highly recommended also is *Postmodernism: Jameson: Critique,* ed. Douglas Kellner (Washington, D.C.: Maisonneuve Press, 1989), which has many stimulating essays about Jameson's theories. A useful comparative study is William C. Dowling, *Jameson, Althusser, Marx* (Ithaca: Cornell University Press, 1984). Finally, for those who want to learn more of the transnational intellectual phenomena so widely active in the 1970s and afterwards, Robert G. Holub's book *Crossing Borders: Reception Theory, Poststructuralism, Deconstruction* (Madison: University of Wisconsin Press, 1992), will have interest.

For a useful introduction to feminist intellectual history, see Rosemarie Tong's *Feminist Thought: An Introduction* (Boulder: Westview Press, 1989). For more on the aspect of feminist theory treated in this book, *Making a Difference: Feminist Literary Criticism,* ed. Gayle Greene and Coppelia Kahn (London: Methuen, 1985) has nine helpful essays. Also, *The New Feminist Criticism: Essays on Women, Literature, and Theory,* ed. Elaine Showalter (New York: Pantheon Books, 1985) contains some major texts. Yet another collection is *Feminist Issues in Literary Scholarship,* ed. Shari Benstock (Bloomington: Indiana University Press, 1987), which has fourteen essays from the 1980s. Two works that I used for the chapter on feminist literary theory are Toril Moi, *Sexual/Textual Politics: Feminist Literary Theory* (London: Methuen, 1985), which deals with the Anglo-American resistance to French theory and follows through to the accommodation achieved in the 1980s, and Janet Todd, *Feminist Literary History* (New York: Routledge, 1988). Those who would like to explore this subject beyond literary criticism into other academic fields should consult *The Impact of Feminist Research in the Academy,* ed. Christie Farnham (Bloomington: Indiana University Press, 1987), which discusses anthropology, history, psychology, science, economics, sociology, and literature. And for the wider feminist movement in the United States, see the appropriate volumes in the Twayne Series, American Women in the Twentieth Century. The volumes to date are Dorothy M. Brown, *Setting a Course: American Women in the*

1920s; Susan Ware, *Holding Their Own: American Women in the 1930s*; Susan M. Hartman, *The Home Front and Beyond: American Women in the 1940s*; Eugenia Kaledin, *Mothers and More: American Women in the 1950s*; and Winifred D. Wandersee, *On the Move: American Women in the 1970s*.

As indicated in the text, the 1970s flourished with many movements in painting, of which we sampled but a few. For brief reviews of these movements see Edward Lucie-Smith, *Art in the Seventies* (Ithaca: Cornell University Press, 1980) and *Artspeak: A Guide to Contemporary Ideas, Movements, and Buzzwords*, by Robert Atkins (New York: Abbeville Publishers, 1990). *The Object of Performance: The American Avant-Garde since 1970*, by Henry M. Sayre (Chicago: University of Chicago Press, 1989) treats of art movements associated with leftist social and political intentions. Providing a wide context for recent painting is Kim Levin, *Beyond Modernism: Essays on Art from the 70s and 80s* (New York: Harper & Row, 1988). For a comprehensive overview of photo-Realism, see Louis K. Meisel, *Photo-Realism* (New York: Abradale Press, 1980).

For architecture, there are several general histories, but for helpful considerations of postmodernism I suggest a look at *The Critical Edge: Controversy in Recent American Architecture*, ed. Tod A. Marder, which has excellent essays on specific important architectural pieces, including several not discussed in the chapter. Also helpful is Beverly Russell, *Architecture and Design, 1970-1990: New Ideas in America* (New York: Harry N. Abrams, 1989). For both architecture and painting the casual and the serious student will find it helpful to look through the many fine art journals that cover a great array of subjects and personalities. Consult *Arts Magazine, Arts, Artforum, Art in America*, and the *Journal of the American Institute of Architects*.

For the long background of conservative thought in America, see Ronald Lora, *Conservative Minds in America* (Chicago: Rand-McNally, 1971). George Nash's *The Conservative Intellectual Movement in America: Since 1945* (New York, 1976) surveys the wide range of conservative opinion over three decades in impressive fashion. J. David Hoeveler, Jr., *Watch on the Right: Conservative Intellectuals in the Reagan Era* (Madison: University of Wisconsin Press, 1991) has chapter studies of eight prominent thinkers. See also William B. Hixson, Jr., *Search for the American Right Wing: An Analysis of the Social Science Record, 1955-1957* (Princeton: Princeton University Press, 1992), which studies various interpretations of conservative political and social movements. Other studies bring conservatism closer to the political arena, especially Jerome L. Himmelstein, *To the Right: The Transformation of American Conservatism* (Berkeley and Los Angeles: University of California Press, 1990), E. J. Dionne, Jr., *Why Americans Hate Politics* (New York: Simon & Schuster, 1991), which is much better than its unfortunate title would suggest, and Gary Dorrien, *The Neoconservative Mind: Politics, Culture, and the War of Ideology* (Philadelphia: Temple University Press, 1993). For a treatment of conservatism from a "paleoconservative" viewpoint, see Paul Gottfried, *The Conservative Movement* (New York: Twayne Publishers, 1993).

Those who wish to have more critical assessments of two important liberal thinkers, John Rawls and Richard Rorty, might begin with two fine anthologies that offer intense readings. See *Reading Rawls: Critical Studies on Rawls' 'A Theory of Justice,'* ed. Norman Daniels (Stanford: Stanford University Press, 1989); and *Reading Rorty: Critical Responses to Philosophy and the Mirror of Nature (and Beyond)*, ed. Alan R. Malachowski (Oxford: Basil Blackwell, 1990). See also Chandran Kukathas and Philip Pettit, *Rawls: A Theory of Justice and Its Critics* (Stanford: Stanford University Press, 1990).

Index

Pages in Italics indicate an extended analysis of the subject.

About the Author

J. David Hoeveler, Jr., teaches American history at the University of Wisconsin–Milwaukee, where he joined the department in 1971. He is the author of three previous books: *The New Humanism: A Critique of Modern America, 1900-1940* (1977); *James McCosh and the Scottish Intellectual Tradition: From Glasgow to Princeton* (1981); and *Watch on the Right: Conservative Intellectuals in the Reagan Era* (1991).